The Self-Sufficient City

Vicente Guallart

I1: Self-sufficiency

Human beings are self-sufficient in that we are part of a habitat.

In the 21st century, our self-sufficiency is on a global level.

Human beings need to produce food, energy and things in order to live.

Each person, each community, each society, each generation throughout history has built its own habitat with the aim of satisfying a particular way of life.

With strong citizens, comes strong society.

Connected self-sufficiency allows for better resilience to global collapse.

I2: City

The Internet has changed our lives, but it hasn't changed our cities, yet.

In the wake of the 20th century worker-consumer, the 21st century belongs to the entrepreneur-producer.

The challenge for the cities of the 21st century has to do with a return to productivity.

We live in a world of cities.

Cities are the actual places where people live and they are the locus of the real economy.

From the centralized model of resource management characteristic of the industrial age, we are moving toward the distributed model of the information society.

The cities and territories that will be leaders in the near future will be the ones that can create value for the surrounding territory using a minimum of resources.

If we understand the economy of the information society to be based on innovation, current urban design is not a part of that economy.

A new metabolic layer needs to be added to the physical and functional layers of cities.

Many slow cities inside a smart city.

Every person lives in a different city.

Any action tied in with the fact of inhabiting is carried out on multiple scales, at a number of different moments, in a continuous system that is adapted to our social reality.

Space is condensed into objects, and objects are becoming smaller every day.

Human beings wouldn't need houses or cities if they wanted living naked out in the middle of nature.

Good architecture and good cities are those that have emerged as part of the history of a specific place on the planet, like a part of nature.

The anatomy of the city, its entire structure, can be organized according to environment, infrastructures, public space, built domain, information and citizens.

1. Dwelling

A dwelling is the central piece in a person's habitability.

If a house is a computer. Its structure is the net.

In the wake of commercial Internet and social Internet, the Internet of things emerges, and by extension, the Internet of cities.

Computers disappear, images expand in space.

Every object and every building in the world will have a digital identity, an IP adress.

We want to upload the physical world onto the Internet.

Every object on the planet has a material history and a formal genealogy.

Dwellings can connect people, instead of keeping them apart.

2. Building

Architecture is the art of dwelling.

Whereas the 20th century saw the transformation of the physical structure of buildings, in the 21st century, buildings will incorporate a metabolism of their own.

Electrification will be to the physical world what digitalization has been to the information world.

Whereas in the 19th century, value was added to the territory by transforming agricultural land into urban land, in the 21st century we can add more value to the territory by regenerating cities in order to make them self-sufficient.

Build cheap, sell high, and hit the road, is over.

In a services economy, the business is to stay.

Form follows energy.

Buildings should be produced artificially and managed naturally.

In order for buildings to be self-sufficient, buildings need to be intelligent.

We have to build buildings like organisms, cities like natural systems.

3. City Block

The dwelling is still at work.

The self-sufficient city block will work
by applying the distributed model of the
Internet to energy and water networks.

Someone who manufactures a chair obtains
the object and retains the knowledge of how
to make it.

Anyone should be able to make anything,
anywhere in the world, sharing knowledge
via a network and making use of local
resources.

Man is like a biochemical machine.

4. Neighborhood

Within the city, neighborhoods are the
organs in the built body.
Neighborhoods are physiological structures
that define the territory that a person can
cover in a natural, repetitive way.

People don't live in their houses.
They inhabit a set of spaces in their
apartment, building, neighborhood or
city, which allow for them to satisfy their
essential needs individually and collectively.

An urban environment can be created
without a traditional city form, with density
and functional diversity.

A group of houses together does not make
a community.

5. Public Space

There are cities in the world where social and economic progress is materialized in public space, in the infrastructures for collective use.

The reinformation of cities promotes a re-engineering process that will allow them to be more efficient.

The dense city is a paradigm for the desire to coexist peacefully.

Cities have always been built on top of themselves.

In the information society, we live simultaneously in different spaces and times.

The networked society allows for simultaneously building a high-speed global system and a low-speed local one.

Every civilization surpasses its predecessor by using less energy and managing more information.

In order to make cities more efficient, we need to increase the resolution of the information we have about them.

6. City

The city is informed energy.

Cities, like organizations, have their own know-how.

Cities, like living beings, have been subject to natural selection.

Every city has an urban clock that marks the progress of its functional development.

The best way to conserve heritage is to augment it.

Each new urban era carries with it an associated economic model (and vice versa).

We are facing a shift from a product-oriented economy to a service-oriented economy.

A city is an idea. It is the sum total of all of the ideas of the people who inhabit it.
The industrial neighborhoods that exist in cities are a dysfunction that is characteristic of 20th century urban design.

The refoundation of cities redefines their geographic centers.

We live in a world of cities. Cities are the places where people live and die.

In the 19th century, the planet was governed by empires and the 20th century was the century of nation-states. The 21st century will be the century of cities.

Cities no longer want to consume what industry has to offer them. Sharing common standards allows for accelerating the processes of innovation and industrial development.

Every city cannot be a world in itself.

The City Protocol should create a system for evaluating cities and a knowledge platform worthy of the information age.

7. Metropolis

Never before in the history of humanity has there been more knowledge about cities, yet they have never been built in such a vulgar way.

Within the same city there are different urban clocks.

In order for there to be more nature in cities, there needs to be less use of public space for private mobility.

After decades of building infrastructures for mobility, logistics and the urbanization of the flat land near rivers, we need to give back to nature part of what urbanization has destroyed.

Cities need to be designed as systems made up of closed cycles for the exchange of energy and information.

We need to educate human beings as people and in their capacity for producing locally the resources they need to live and sharing globally the knowledge they accumulate: people, surroundings, planet.

We shift from a model where cities receive products and generate trash, to a model where the only thing entering and leaving cities is information, and their resources are produced locally. From "products in, trash out" to "data in, data out".

Epilogue: From Metapolis to Hyperhabitat

The Metapolis is a discontinuous metropolis

The connected self-sufficient city changes the scale of governance of the world and brings us closer to a city-state model, within continental federations.

I_1

SELF-SUFFICIENCY

This is the image: Imagine a primitive man living in a cave. He builds a fire at night to keep warm and fashions a flint arrowhead in the firelight, which he will use to hunt when the dawn comes. On the other side of the cave, another man dips his hands into animal blood or pigment; he draws an animal on the wall in a ritual before the hunt. These are self-sufficient men. They produce the energy, tools and food they need to survive. And they invoke the profound depths of humanity to inspire their existence.

Human beings are self-sufficient in that we are part of a habitat. We are born, we live, we reproduce and we die, like all living things do. We are part of habitable environment, the functional extension of which has changed throughout history. We have been able to create habitable structures even in most unfavorable conditions. In the coldest regions of the planet, the Inuit community has carried on for centuries using the resources they could obtain from their most immediate surrounding and they have adapted their lifestyle, like all species in nature, to their ecosystem. Local self-sufficiency. In the 21st century, our self-sufficiency is global. We don't know where the energy we consume comes from, or the clothes we wear, or the food we eat. A large number of human beings function merely as part of a system that was implemented decades ago. We don't know why our world is the way it is. We just live in it. We have been taught in keeping with its rules, and we have been taught how to follow them. On too many occasions, Man is a supporting actor in his own life. As a part of his natural history, our primitive man had children. Those children had children, and more children, and so on. Let's imagine that one of those descendents is at the Atlanta airport, one of the biggest airports in the world, and he's missed his connecting flight. If he wants to catch the next plane to his destination, a machine will decide when and how he'll do it.

If he asks someone for information, he'll be directed to a screen or someone will type his name into a computer and the machine will provide an answer. The self-sufficient hunter's descendant, today, is simply a machine operator. He doesn't make decisions; he pushes buttons and works as part of a system that someone invented, programmed and installed. A biological robot, of sorts. He can subsist as part of a global system, the planet as a whole, but all by himself he wouldn't know how to produce energy, or food, or the things he needs to survive. At present, he just pushes buttons. However, the information society can connect people in distant places, who share knowledge of the highest level, which can be used to produce the resources necessary for their lives.

Let's imagine a young scientist leading an international working session over a video conference call. She is interacting with twenty communities of entrepreneurs who are preparing to produce a microcontroller to build a network of sensors that will be installed in the areas near where they live in order to collect environmental data on their surroundings. After the virtual meeting, one of the young participants will head to the roof of his building to pick vegetables that he has planted there and watered with the building's recycled water. The same young man will produce a piece of furniture with digital manufacturing machines, using wood from a nearby forest where every tree is geo-referenced. The rest of the wood will be used to produce electricity and hot water in a biomass generator, constructed from a kit produced in his lab using a file downloaded from the Internet.

This human being, a far-off descendent of a cave-dweller, has a highly local domain of self-sufficiency and produces as many local resources as he can because of the knowledge he shares globally across information networks.

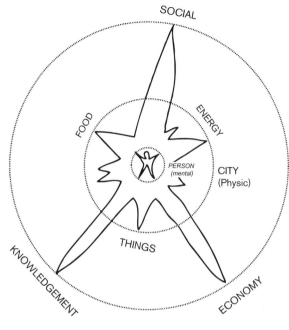

SOCIAL

ENERGY

FOOD

PERSON
(mental)

CITY
(Physic)

PLANET
(Information)

THINGS

KNOWLEDGEMENT

ECONOMY

The connected self-sufficient
man (the same diagram could
be applied to cities).

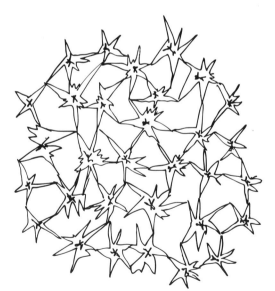

The World: a collaborative network
of self-sufficient networks (the
same diagram could be applied to
connected self-sufficient cities).

Everyone configures their own particular habitat through their daily actions and through the resources they generate and consume, whether it is an aboriginal community in the jungle, a mountain village, a neighborhood in a European city, an American suburb or an Asian megalopolis. Each person, each community, each society, each generation throughout history has built its own habitat with the aim of satisfying a particular way of life. At the beginning of the 21st century we have the possibility of rewriting our history and the history of our urban habitat using the knowledge and the resources at our disposal in order to produce the resources we need to live locally. Energy, food and goods.

A new human being emerges as a result of access to universal knowledge, used for individual purposes and for the good of the community. Knowledge that allows for producing resources locally, while participating in global social networks of knowledge and economy. The strongest societies are made up of individuals with strong leadership abilities and the desire to share.

With strong citizens, comes strong society.

This book is an attempt at defining the conditions in the urban environment that will allow the cities of the 21st century to be inhabited in networked self-sufficiency. Conditions that will make it possible for human beings to take charge of the organization of their existence. The project is centered on rehumanizing cities based on efficiency in the generation and consumption of resources and the creation of people's quality of life, promoting local culture, from a global technological and economic foundation. A new economy of urban innovation.

Cities, which have hidden their obsolescence in recent years behind spectacular formal artifices in the form of architectural icons, have the ability to rewrite their history using new principles that emerge from the distributed systems favored by the information society. This model surpasses the centralized systems from the industrial society by building new functional structures and social structures based on the relationship between multiple entities which act in the form of a network.

Connected self-sufficiency allows for better resistance to global collapse. In times of crisis, like the present, guaranteeing the supply of resources and the safety of the development of urban processes is as important as the processes themselves. Distributed systems, which are the result of the interaction of self-sufficient units, are more flexible and adaptable to change. They have a reduced impact on the territory, on mobility and on the consumption of systemic resources because they use local resources. With increased self-sufficiency in the multiple layers of the management of our habitat, comes increased decision-making capability concerning the kind of habitable spaces and pace of life we wish to develop.

This text asserts that it is possible to regenerate the city into a habitable ecosystem based on the local production of resources and the global connection of knowledge, using new principles and technologies belonging to the information age. This process generates new kinds of buildings, urban spaces, neighborhoods or urban networks to create an urban habitat conceived of from the standpoint of a new discipline, emerging from the fusion of urban design, the environment and information networks. The aim of the process is to promote the well-being of people and communities based on new, more natural and social ways of life, put together by citizens, organizations and cities themselves.

A global city of cities.

A connected self-sufficient city.

I_2

CITY

Internet has changed our lives, but it hasn't changed our cities, yet. In the 21st century, networks allow us to access nearly any piece of information produced by other human beings which, if it is properly managed, can produce knowledge.

How will cities and habitats be able to extract knowledge from the network and produce resources locally in the new society that is emerging with the information age? Cities and the human habitat are the reflection of the culture of each period. They use knowledge and technological advances to create the most effective living conditions from an economic, social and environmental point of view, using the resources within their reach in a rational way.

In the 20th century, work specialization was promoted to increase efficiency and produce more using fewer resources, but along the way a lot of the things that make us human were forgotten. The history is well known. A large segment of the population became workers in a mass-production system that became increasingly globalized and centralized. At the same time, they became consumers of the resources produced by that system. And cities were transformed to adapt to that reality.

Internet promotes a distributed system for the management of reality, where each node in the network is capable of producing and interchanging resources. In this way, by participating actively in global economic and social networks, as well as knowledge networks, a citizen or an organization can produce local resources using the knowledge generated using the network.

After the worker-consumers of the 20th century, comes the entrepreneur-producers of the 21st century, who take charge of their own professional activities within flexible organizations. But "cities of knowledge" will need to be transformed into some more than just a slogan. Knowledge is used to make and do things.

The challenge for cities in the 21st century is becoming productive again. To do that, they need to modify their physical and functional structure in order to produce most of the resources they need locally, while they remain hyperconnected with the world.

Cities are the actual places where people live and where the real economy is produced. The shape of the city follows the shape of the economy that supports it, in accordance with the rules that govern each territory. As such, in order to transform the economy, cities need to be transformed first.

Global warming, the peak in oil consumption, the electrification of the world, social networks, the knowledge of complex systems, and the global economic crisis are all part of a transition process that should instigate the construction of a new economic and urban paradigm for the world. Cities cannot be habitable centers that merely consume nature's limited resources. The era of infinite resources is over. Cities are habitable ecosystems, which are part of a global system, and they need to be analyzed as such. The cities and territories that will be leaders in the near future will be the ones that can create value for the surrounding territory using a minimum of resources.

As such, a new model must be defined for the organization of cities in the information society based on self-sufficient structures on different scales. Cities and their nearby surroundings should produce the energy, the goods and the food they need to sustain human life.

In order for a multiscalar system of habitability to be self-sufficient, each of its scales needs to tend toward self-sufficiency: self-sufficient buildings, in self-sufficient neighborhoods, within self-sufficient districts to create a self-sufficient city within the framework of a self-sufficient region, where everyone is connected

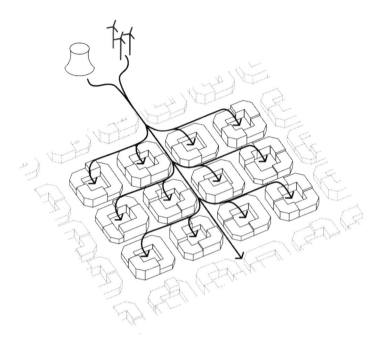

via information networks. Each of the scales and territorial settings should develop its potential to the fullest and compensate for its needs with resources from the closest scale or setting.

Throughout human history, each change in the energy cycle has produced different types of human habitats.

Human beings were initially hunter-gatherers; later they organized into agricultural communities which gave rise to the first civilizations; from there, the first stable settlements were developed in the form of fortified cities, which, in many cases, served as the origin of the cities we now know. With the industrial revolution, real systematic urban development began, which, for over a hundred and fifty years, has allowed for the construction of our present-day cities. The industrial economy has developed well in places where there are raw materials or energy sources, or where there is a suitable workforce and enough human capital to allow for the production of goods. Now, in the information society, the multiscalar city that spans from a single home to the entire planet should base its economy on the trade of knowledge and services on a global scale and on the local production of material goods using a maximum of local resources.

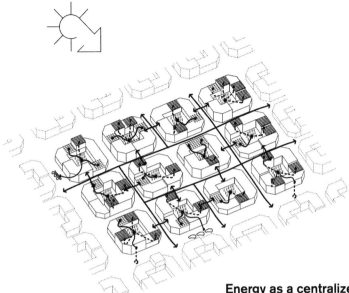

**Energy as a centralized system
versus a distributed system.
The Internet of Energy.**

Towards Barcelona 5.0

Barcelona has seen all of the phases of the construction of a dense
European city that has grown in concentric rings over time. It was
founded by the Romans on a small hill near the sea around the
year 15 BC and was given the name Barcino. It was sustained by
agriculture; it had a surface area of some 12 hectares and it was
surrounded by a wall that was 1.5 km long.

That was Barcelona 1.0.

That city and its walls underwent a number of modifications and
enlargements until the Middle Ages, when the consolidation of the
Crown of Aragon by Jaume I led to the construction of a city to
serve as the capital of an empire that would stretch out across the
Mediterranean. A city that was the product of feudal society, where
craftsmen and trade guilds emerged and trade flourished both
by land and by sea. In 1250 a new wall was built, which would be
extended in the 15th century to reach a length of six kilometers and
to enclose an area of some 218 hectares.

That was Barcelona 2.0.

The industrial revolution, which occurred as a result of developments in science and technology along with the use of new kinds of energy and the invention of mechanical pulling power, sparked the beginning of the industrial city and, with it, the development of the territory. At the same time the universal declaration of the rights of man brought forth a new consciousness about people's living conditions. Barcelona beginning tearing down the city walls in 1854, based on a plan intended to increase the surface area of the city by tenfold. That was Barcelona 3.0

A utopian socialist, Ildefons Cerdà[1], invented the concept of urban design with the plan for Barcelona's Eixample. Cerdà planned a city with surface area dedicated to transportation as well as green areas and spaces for building. Cerdà's urban planning was based on a utopian vision of the construction of a territory, which attempted to take advantage of the technological potential of the period and its collectivization, while responding to the new living conditions required by emerging industrial society. The project was intended to provide better quality of life for city-dwellers by creating a more hygienic and healthy city, a city where the buildings would open onto green areas and where sunlight would filter in through the windows. The construction of the Eixample continued for a period of 150 years.

During that time, a new technology, the automobile, which began consistent industrial development during the 1920s, allowed for the development of new more disperse forms of cities, initially in the United States, and has come to transform the pace of life in historic cities and their operations. In the case of Barcelona, this new technology prompted the construction of a perimeter ring road in 1992 (based on the example of Paris in the 1970s), with a length of 32 kilometers and enclosing a surface area of 1,000

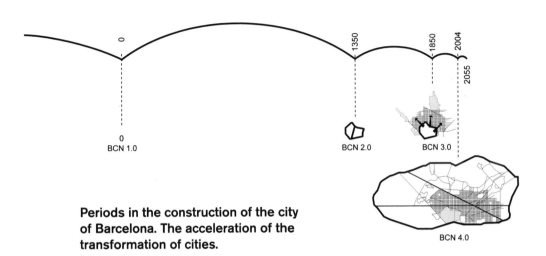

**Periods in the construction of the city
of Barcelona. The acceleration of the
transformation of cities.**

hectares, and a second ring road that organizes the metropolitan
area, with a length of 60 kilometers and an interior surface area of
25,000 hectares. It marks the end of the period characterized by an
urban development model based on the occupation of farmland or
obsolete industrial areas and the beginning of the regeneration of
the information city brought on by digital technology.
That was Barcelona 4.0.
The coming years should be dedicated to developing and
implementing this model, first through prototype projects and then
in a massive, comprehensive fashion. Between 2050 and 2060, the
city should be self-sufficient in terms of energy, and the economy of
local production should have been developed, along with the global
interchange of designs, solutions and services.
That will be Barcelona 5.0.
The present crisis is driving a change in how we live and work.
Initially, urban design was a science created to add value to a
territory by transforming farmland, used for producing food, into
urban territory, where people could work and live in a much denser

and more economically productive environment. Today, however, the process of urban planning has become more of a technical mechanism than a strategic one. A large number of cities are being managed in response to political or economic circumstances, without a vision focused on development in the medium or long term City planning no longer adds much value to the territory. It has become a mechanism for regulating the relationships between public and private space, used for economic profit while adding minimum objective value to the territory, organizing the obvious. If we understand the economy of the information society to be based on innovation, current urban design is not a part of that economy. For now.

How can we add value to cities?
Whereas urban design in the 19th century added value to agricultural land to transform it into urban land, the regeneration of the city begun in the 21st century adds value to urban land by making it self-sufficient.
A new metabolic layer needs to be added to the physical and functional layers of cities, that can incorporate the management of the resources those cities need in order to operate. Cities cannot be places that transform products into trash, environments that only consume resources that are brought in from the outside. Energy needs to be produced locally by recycling buildings and neighborhoods. Goods need to be produced in urban environments using clean industry and food needs to be produced ecologically in cities or in nearby areas. A new informational layer needs to be added to cities to allow for the distributed management of all urban networks.
We need to promote a new model for networked cities made up of self-sufficient, productive neighborhoods that move at human

speed, within a hyperconnected, zero-emissions city.
A model that incorporates the best aspects of the quality of life
in small cities and the best aspects of urban density and the
dynamism of big cities in the information society.
Many slow cities inside a smart city.

Rather than adding an informational layer on top of an obsolete
city, new ways of organizing urban space should be promoted,
functional hybridization and ways of dealing with mobility that
make cities more efficient from a structural perspective. Internet
should not draw out the life of cities as we know them now; it
should allow for their re-engineering.
First, however, we should define the anatomy of cities as a shared,
common foundation on which to operate. It is unbelievable that
we have gone on for more than five thousand years building cities
without any international conventions to define the structure of a city.
If we ask a doctor in Lima, in Paris, or in Bombay what systems
make up the human body, they will all describe the circulatory
system, the nervous system, the respiratory system and all the
various systems that constitute human anatomy, and which
are studied at medical schools throughout the world. However,
architects in those same cities will give different description of the
parts or the systems that make up the anatomy of a city.
Clearly defining the parts of a system is the first step toward
remodeling it.

(In Europe, urban design will never again be a mechanism for
constructing the territory in an abstract natural context. At present,
any construction is a reaction to an existing reality, whether urban
or natural. Outside of cities, as opposed to building in nature, we

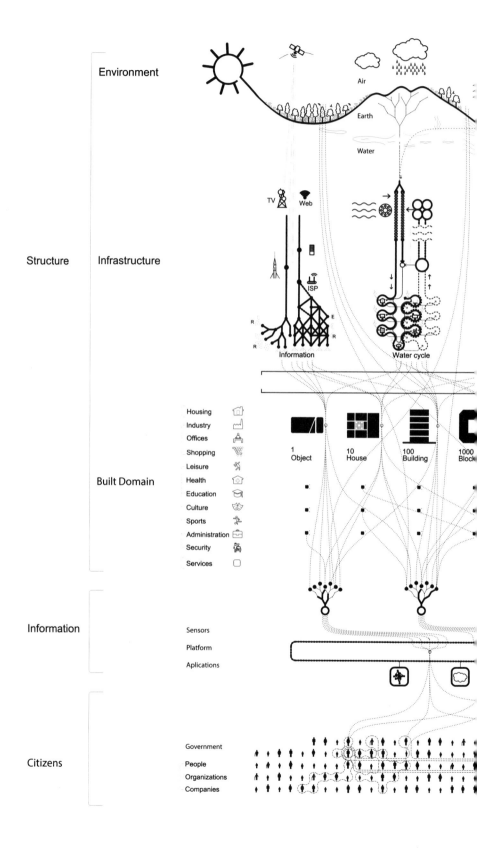

Environment

Structure

Infrastructure

Air

Earth

Water

TV

Web

ISP

E

R

R

R

Information

Water cycle

Built Domain

Housing

Industry

Offices

Shopping

Leisure

Health

Education

Culture

Sports

Administration

Security

Services

1
Object

10
House

100
Building

1000
Block

Information

Sensors

Platform

Aplications

Citizens

Government

People

Organizations

Companies

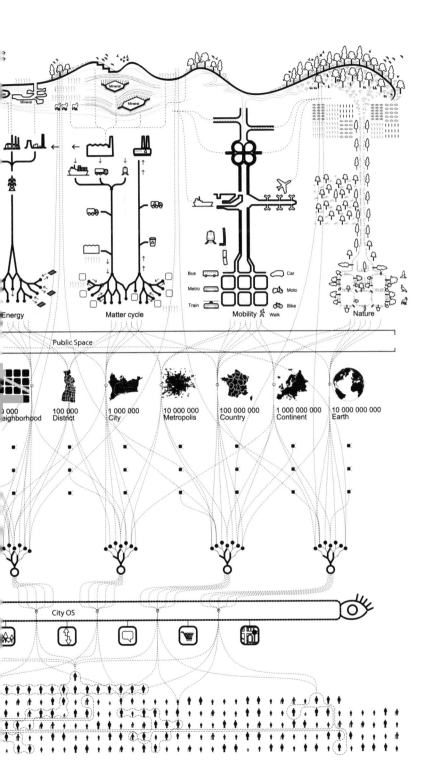

The anatomy of a city: Structure, (Environment, Infrastructures and Built Domain), Information and People.

will be building with nature. Or better yet, building nature itself. The greatest challenge for our civilization lies in reforming the cities that have already been built, which are home to more than 50% of the world's population, in order to increase their efficiency, make them more productive, and to ensure that the new cities that will be built in the coming years, especially in Asia or Africa, will be based on new principles that are in keeping with the information society. If all new cities are built according to current models, when the planet reaches 10 billion inhabitants, in 2050 according to predictions, there will not be enough material energy to sustain its activity.

We are faced with the challenge of a new rebirth for cities, built on their historic and social history, by way of a new, more transparent, open and participative culture, where citizens will be the leading figures in the story, in the framework of a society that works, is productive, and can debate about its own progress. Cities that are built as declarations of the excellence of human creation.

A connected self-sufficient city.

I_3

NETWORK

How is a city like a network? Are cities compatible with the information society's network model?

A city concentrate an incredible accumulation of information and activities in its territory. However, the mechanisms we use to organize cities seem totally obsolete. Any section of the city is defined according to its form and its function. Volumetric information and a type of use. We don't know anything about how it works, its metabolism, its behavior or its relationship to surrounding areas.

In 2001, a group of architects and scientists from Barcelona created the Master's Degree in Advanced Architecture in collaboration with the Universitat Politècnica de Catalunya (UPC) and the Massachusetts Institute of Technology (MIT), which would later serve as the foundation for the creation of the Institute for Advanced Architecture of Catalonia (IAAC), which I directed until I became chief architect for the Barcelona City Council in 2011. The architects Willy Muller, Manuel Gausa, the anthropologist Artur Serra and the engineer Sebastià Sallent were co-promoters of the center, which collaborated from the outset with MIT's Center for Bits and Atoms, directed by Neil Gershenfeld.

One of the areas of our research was directed toward developing a model that would allow us to take on a global vision of cities and the world that would allow for reprogramming cities globally based on the model of a network.

A city like a network.

We were looking for a model for analyzing cities that would be compatible with the topology of the Internet. A model where the Internet and the city could be fused together. I had to be a multiscalar and self-similar model, like a fractal system, where the parts have the same shape as the whole. It had to be applicable to a living environment for one person or for 10 billion people. It had to be compatible with the concept of a dwelling-city and that of a planet-city. Traditionally, urban planning has been understood as the large-scale project that allows for organizing the territory in order to build cities. Architecture is derived from it, tasked with developing the design for the scale of the buildings and, later, the design of their interiors. The networks of services are applied on top, developed with an understanding of civil, industrial or telecommunications engineering. However, a multiscalar vision of human habitability analyzes and designs all of the scales on which people live with the same intensity and within the same overall project. And they are all developed according to similar principles and parameters, applying specific questions in each case.

A multi-scalar and self-similar design of the human habitat.

Today, the ordering of cities happens primarily in two dimensions: the space where buildings can be constructed, with associated uses, and open space. And within them, the spaces dedicated to mobility and green areas. The density of land available for building is clearly defined in a number of cities, as a way of associating an economic productivity with the land. In others, especially in English-speaking areas, it can be an object of negotiation.

The Master Plan for Barcelona uses 29 categories toward the classification of any piece of land in the city, ranging from housing to cemeteries and green areas. Many American cities based on zoning use a good deal fewer.

How is it possible that, as well as we can understand a city, the regulations are organized and defined according to so few parameters? In the investigation titled *Hyperhabitat* [2], carried out in conjunction with Daniel Ibáñez and Rodrigo Rubio beginning in 2006, we analyzed the work carried out at different educational centers dealing with city design in which parameters from different categories were mixed together.

Like in *Sim City*, a classic in the history of video games, used in a number of universities throughout the world as a pedagogical system, the idea was to build a city beginning with a blank map, which the player was expected to fill, expand and manage on a set budget. The city had to include all the basic services and facilities: an aqueduct, public transportation, electricity, urban waste management, etc. Players also had to provide for access to healthcare and education, security and leisure activities for all inhabitants.

Salvador Rueda[3], director of Barcelona's Urban Ecology Agency, had a very intelligent approach to the question of the functional organization of the city in order to determine its degree of "diversity". He studied the National Classification of Economic Activities (CNAE), divided into 17 wide groups (construction, commerce, education, etc.), which include 766 different headings, and the Tax on Economic Activities (IAE) which includes 1,059 headings classified into three general sections (business activities, professional activities and artistic activities) and used them to develop an even more extensive system based on 7 categories with a total of 2,000 different headings or activities. Using the appropriate information, he mapped all of the activities that are carried out in the city on top of the plan of the different plots. That was how he was able to define the urban complexity index, which recognizes which parts of the city are more diverse and complex from the standpoint of the city's functional ecosystem. The more diverse a part of the city is, the better.

Those are the kind of figures that are characteristic of our times.

How can a city be comparable to a network? How can a planet-city
be comparable to the Internet?

A network is made up of nodes for storage and for computation, connections that transmit the information, an environment or a medium
in which they can take place, and information including the protocols
that govern them.

Nodes, connections, environment and information.

If we imagine a planet before the first human settlements, we can
picture a natural environment occupied by living things that are
established in different geological structures and ecosystems.
This territory was traversed by the first human beings who lived
in caves. As men travelled across the territory, they began tracing
the first networks of roads, recognizing the places that were easier
to access. From the first settlements, the first villages were created,
often for defensive reasons.

Those fixed nodes in the territory ended up consolidating the
communication routes created as a result of the principle of
minimum effort. The first connections between stable nodes
served to fix the migrations toward territories where there were
animals to hunt and, later on, with the birth of cities, to define the
transportation routes for people and goods.

Many of the cities we know today emerged based on settlements
organized by colonizing civilizations for the control of territory, for
trade, in the intersection of roads, on farms, or around functional
attractors that promoted economic development. Throughout
history, protocols for interaction have been constructed on top
of those connected nodes (whether for trade, the exploitation
of resources, or for defense) in order to define internal rules for
operation and for interactions with other nodes.

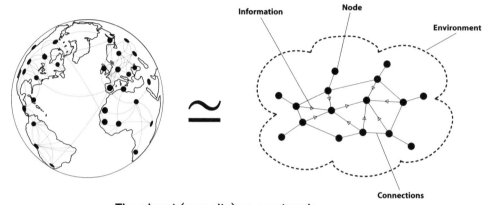

The planet (or a city) as a network.

What is the smallest city on Earth? What is the difference between a city and a rural settlement where people, live, work, rest and sometimes trade? In the same way, we might ask ourselves, what is the basic function that serves to define a place as a dwelling? Is it a place to rest, to seek shelter or to store goods?

Every individual lives in a different city.

People don't live in dwellings. We live in a continuous system of different-scaled functional nodes which allow us to carry out our daily activities. We live on the planet and carry out the functions we desire in order to develop as people, in our homes, in our neighborhoods, in cities, in a region, or globally. We carry out every action that is characteristic of the act of inhabiting on multiple scales, at a number of different moments, in a continuous system that is adapted to our social reality.

We can eat at home alone, in a small group, in a restaurant, or at a banquet, but we have to eat. We can educate ourselves by reading books, attending classes, going to university or participating in conferences. We rest in the shade of a tree, in the yard outside our house, in a public park, or in a national park. We can engage in physical activity individually, running on a treadmill, or we can run in a popular marathon with fifty thousand other people. And we can watch the Olympic Games on television, together with a billion other people.

We carry out the activities that we wish to engage in each day through structure that are for individual, collective or global use. As such, it is worthwhile to think about how to organize the city for each individual in a multi-scalar system comprised of dwelling, city, planet (with all of the intermediate scales), and how to define a multi-scalar matrix for the development of human life. That is how we can recognize nodes in the territory (from a dwelling to a city) and networks that connect them (for mobility and for utilities) organized in a physical environment, and information produced in any interaction between them.

Nodes, connection, environment and information.

NODES (BUILT DOMAIN)

Any object or structure that carries out a function for human life is a functional node that can have its own identity in the global network.

During the 20th century, the industrialization process transformed many spaces and objects. Many appliances and machines for use in homes have condensed different activities in one machine, which used to be carried out in spaces that generated a certain amount of social activity in the vicinity. The washing machine eliminated public laundries in village squares. The drier put an end to activity on the roofs of buildings. Other machines have meant that actions involving crossing spaces have been transformed into domestic machines, like stationary bicycles and treadmills, etc.

Space is condensed by objects. And objects are becoming smaller every day. At the limit, they become computer applications. Many of the objects that exist in a home are possible because they are a part of a larger-scale network made up of other elements and systems and, as the case may be, buildings. A refrigerator makes sense because of the entire cold chain. A refrigerator on the scale of one person is a small appliance. For ten people, we could find a family format, with a double door. For a hundred people, one can be found in any small restaurant. For a thousand people, they exist in supermarkets, and supply lower-level refrigerators. For ten thousand, in a large shopping center or a big hotel, and, more than machines, they are climate-controlled rooms. For a hundred thousand or a million people, we have large refrigerated logistics centers, in the central markets in large cities.

In the same way, on the other extreme from the existence of an individual outlet, there is an electricity network, a nuclear power plant or a wind farm. A toilet, and a sewer treatment plant.

A personal library in someone's home is fed by a bookstore, or a library, which may be a neighborhood library for ten thousand users or a country's national library or the U.S. Library of Congress. Every object belongs to a functional category, which, as it increases in scale, can become a building. Or a city. A small crucifix relates to a chapel, which can relate to a neighborhood church, or a cathedral and, finally, the Vatican. Objects, buildings, cities that encompass everything from the scale of an individual to a billion people. From one Muslim's prayer carpet to Mecca. From a personal printer to a large print shop, to a publishing capital. From a small winery to a large bottling plant for alcoholic beverages.

Based on a model city, we can define the following scales for physically grouping people together:

1 Dwelling
10 Floor
100 Building
1000 City Block
10,000 Neighborhood
100,000 District
1,000,000 City
10,000,000 Region
100,000,000 Country
1,000,000,000 Continent
10,000,000,000 Planet

There are technologies, associated with these functional nodes, which make sense at a particular scale. For example, the nuclear power plants in existence today have the capacity to serve from one to ten million people. But, for now, there aren't any nuclear facilities designed to serve just dozens of people. The scale at which human needs are resolved results in one type of city or another. Objects can be purchased in a small craftsman's shop or a large shopping center. Cities where there are small businesses, normally associated with a historic city center, establish a local kind of commerce with people who can do their shopping on foot. Cities with large shopping centers are dependent on individual modes of transportation, like cars, which are characteristic of American cities, and are used to access those shopping centers from the individual dwellings in surrounding areas. Different city models are defined based on the scales at which individual needs are met, which determines the associated models for mobility, density and social interaction. Every node has a production cost and an operational cost with an economic, social and environmental impact on its environment.

CONNECTIONS (INFRASTRUCTURES)

The connections to a network are infrastructures defined by a constant section and a linear trajectory that connects all of the functional nodes in one category with each other, from object-level to city-level. If we analyze present-day cities, we can observe six vectors or cycles that connect everything with everything else, and which make the territory work. They are: information networks, the water cycle (clean water and waste water), the materials cycle (logistical transportation and waste materials, energy, human transportation and green systems.

In general, the public space, which is a physiological concept related to the use, includes all of these networks in a complex section that includes the underground level. The expansion that occurred during the urbanization process in the 19th century promoted the rationalization of the connections between nodes in cities.

1. Information: For centuries, communications were analog, taking place via messengers and letters. Later, the 20th century saw the emergence of the telegraph, the telephone, radio, television and then, as the paradigm of a new era, the Internet. In contrast to the centralized model of television and radio, where there is one emitter and many receivers, the Internet allows for a distributed organization of information, with many emitters and many receivers. There are telecommunications networks that transport information using copper cables, fiber optic cables and through the electromagnetic spectrum.

2. The water Cycle, consisting of Water supply and Sanitation, the management of clean water and waste water.
Clean water: Water, like all natural elements, has its own cycle, in which it passes through solid, liquid and gaseous states in rivers,

seas and in the atmosphere. It has always been a determining factor in defining human settlements. There can be no life, and no cities, without water. Water for human consumption generally comes from wells and from rivers and lakes, and, currently, from desalinization plants.

Waste water: The separation of human waste using sewer systems was introduced in cities with the urbanization process during the 19th century. For hundreds of years, human waste was dumped into rivers and seas, or used as a part of the nutrient cycle: food-consumption-waste-fertilizer-food. The densification of cities, however, meant that waste had to be carried far away from settlements and later treated, in order to avoid an environmental impact on the surroundings. With the aid of present-day technology, many cities treat their waste water, separating solid waste that is converted into fertilizer, to produce water that can be reintroduced into the consumption cycle. In some cases, the result is grey water, which can be used for agriculture and secondary networks. Clean water and waste water make up the water cycle.

3. The material cycle, consisting of the extraction of resources from nature, their industrial or small-scale manipulation to transform them into products, their logistical transportation to the points of consumption, and the collection of the waste produced during their manipulation.

Logistical transportation: The first human transportation networks were also used for transporting raw materials and goods. However, the transportation of products, especially during the 20th century, has resulted in its own logistical platforms, ports and airport, with specific distribution laws in cities and with specific schedules, routes and management.

Waste material: In the same way the nodes at any scale (dwellings, buildings or cities) are supplied with goods that are transformed into food or are used to produce new goods, the resulting waste material is sent out of the city to be accumulated in landfills or treated for the purpose of creating recycled materials that will again be transformed into new products, or to generate energy. Today, in compact urban centers, there are automatic trash collection systems that automate the process. Logistics and waste materials make up the materials cycle.

4. Energy: At present, energy is produced in large functional nodes, in nuclear plants, wind farms and hydroelectric centers, in solar fields and, increasingly, in buildings. Energy networks transport mainly electricity or natural gas. Oil is transported in large ships or through pipelines to plants that produce diesel fuel or chemical elements. Currently, energy networks have a branching structure, from large production nodes to smaller nodes for domestic and industrial generation.

5. Human transportation: This was, without a doubt, the first network. Roads that were created by many sets of feet. Networks built up by caravans, on the silk road, or by wagonloads of settlers. Sea routes, too. In the city, the street is the setting for people's mobility; today, streets have been segregated in many case by systems that are organized according to vehicle type: pedestrians, bicycles, cars, public transportation, metro, trains, etc. In the United States, the highway system, a mobility network that is segregated from urban areas, was also developed extensively. City streets and squares represent the spaces for human mobility; in traditional cities, they are meeting places where paths cross, and spaces for social interaction.

6. Natural networks. The urbanization process and the construction of streets in the 19th century marked the beginning of the systematic introduction of networks of street trees as an integral part of public space. These networks promote the flow of biological information between different parts of the city, and between the city and its natural environment. Likewise, the natural networks act as environmental regulators of public space, helping to control the sun exposure on the horizontal plane of the city, regulating humidity in public space and improving air quality.

The categories of networks, as such, are limited. Networks connect nodes on different scales and allow them to operate. One urban model or another will imply more or less flow in the networks that operate in the city. Present-day cities organize the networks in a tree-like system, from large production centers (energy, information or water) to consumption points (buildings). Or from small center that generate waste material (dwellings, buildings) to the large centers where they are treated. One urban model or another will imply more or less flow in the networks that operate in the city. A self-sufficient city will develop a system of networks in a grid that will connect many points with a similar weight, and it will eliminate or reduce dependency on large networks that transport resources from large production centers to consumption points.

ENVIRONMENT

Human beings wouldn't need houses or cities if they were interested in living naked out in the middle of nature.
The construction of cities and buildings is a mechanism to control conditions in the environment where we live, and to create stable temperatures and humidity levels throughout the year. The three

fundamental media on the planet are earth, water and air. Their interaction, governed by the position of the Earth with respect to the sun and by the influence of the moon, defines the different climatic conditions and the varied landscapes across the planet. From the poles to the Amazon rainforest. The environmental conditions in a place have always been a fundamental condition to define the potential for living there. Man, as a living being, tries to live in places that require the least expense of energy to obtain necessary resources and create the conditions to support life. Historic settlements, on top of which most cities have developed, were set up rationally, seeking out access to water and protection from the wind as well as possible attacks from the outside.

In China, the discipline of Feng Shui was developed, which allows for choosing the best-suited places according to geographic conditions, first for the purpose of burying the dead and later for founding cities and building houses, relating the shape of the territory and its conditions with the four traditional elements in Eastern culture: earth, water, fire and air. The geomancer was in charge of using this knowledge to choose the locations for settlements. In the present day, those foundational arguments having to do with cities are again determining factors when it comes to using local resources and orienting future development toward self-sufficiency.

The Earth exists as we know it because of the influence of the Sun, around which it orbits and which sends out its rays in the form of light and heat that allowed for the emergence of living beings. Its calorific action serves to define Earth's different climate zones. From the atomic particles that served to form the Earth, different chemical reaction and physical processes created a situation characterized by a certain amount of stability; they created a solid medium, the land, a liquid one, water, and a gaseous one, the air. Life began in the liquid medium, from chemical reactions that resulted in single-cell organisms and, later, more complex ones that set off the history of evolution. Human beings, like all living things, are a part of that chain.

The Earth is the natural environment for human life. It is a medium made up of layers that span from the core to the crust. The rocks and surfaces with which Man interacts have been produced over millions of years through lithological cycles that transform minerals into different kinds of sedimentary, metamorphic or volcanic rock. They are very slow transformation cycles, which can be perceived in real time through tectonic movements in the form of earthquakes or volcanic eruptions. The Earth contains large pockets of hydrocarbons that are insoluble in water, produced by the transformation of organic material over thousands of years. Minerals are extracted from the Earth for the production of all kinds of goods which have been used to build cities throughout history. Water is essential to human life, because living things need water to survive. It covers 71% of the Earth's surface and 97% of it is saltwater. Water moves through the hydrologic cycle in a constant process of evaporation due to the effect of sunlight and subsequent precipitation and run-off across the Earth's surface. Water is present as gaseous water vapor in clouds, as a liquid in seas, lakes and rivers, and as a solid in the polar ice caps and in icebergs. 70% of water consumption on the Earth is for agricultural purposes, 20% for industrial uses and 10% for human consumption. Access to water has always been a condition for founding human settlements, which first began near rivers or lakes. The presence of water in rivers or in the air in cities helps define the environmental conditions for human habitability.

The air is the mixture of gases that make up the Earth's atmosphere. It contains mainly nitrogen and oxygen. The Earth's atmosphere is divided into layers according to altitude. All of the atmospheric phenomena that create our climate are formed in the first layer. In the stratosphere, at a height of 25 kilometers, lies the ozone layer, which protects the Earth from ultraviolet rays and which has been damaged by the effects of greenhouse gases. The air quality in cities, which is a source of growing concern because of its effects on people's health, is evaluated by measuring the amounts of nitrogen dioxide (NO_2), particulate matter (PM-10), tropospheric ozone (O_3), or sulfur dioxide (SO_2).

Good architecture and good cities are those that have emerged as part of the history of a specific place on the planet, like a part of nature. They are the product of civilizations that have built buildings, streets and cities that have been able to relate the culture and the history of a people to the management of the resources within their reach. And they have turned the process into an art form.

Sun, Air, Earth and Water and living systems have shaped the different ecosystems on the planet that people interact with and on which we build our habitats. And this relationship maintained its equilibrium for hundreds of years. However, the industrial revolution and the massive emission of greenhouse gases are causing structural changes in the planet. The historian Dipesh Chakrabarty[4] asserts that Man is no longer a biological being, but a geological one, because his actions in past decades have changed the climate on a global level, in that same way that multiple simultaneous volcanic eruptions could have. Reversing or redirecting this process is only possible by way of actions that can change the essence of the systems we use to interchange energy and information with our environment.

The question we must face is whether this process will be determined by man himself or whether nature will decide it for us by her own means.

INFORMATION
The goal of a network is the exchange of information.
The city is a system of systems. An overlap of material and social structures that are organized to work according to the rules of cohabitation created by the inhabitants.
A city generates trillions of bytes of information that are the result of a conversation, a social event, for the collective construction of the city based on the daily activities of its inhabitants. They are created by people's interactions with the urban system, in the entire physiological layer of the city, in mobility, in commerce, in education and in culture. In the metabolic layer too, when certain infrastructures interact with others, to keep the exchange cycles for materials and information in operation.
A city is a system that involves living beings; that makes it an ecosystem, which includes the physical medium, its inhabitants and the flows of information created between them.
Throughout human history, this exchange of information has taken place in the city analogically. Now, with the advent of the information society, many of these interactions have multiplied and they can be organized, stored and programmed for the benefit of the system as a whole, and for the addition of new potentials. It is the re-information of the city. That is why a new information layer has appeared in Urban Anatomy that didn't exist until a few years ago. This layer is central to the development of the self-sufficient city and to changing the model toward distributed systems.
The great challenge for cities is developing this new information

layer in an integrated way. Until now, many of the urban systems that have come from the industrial world (train, metro, water, mobility, energy) have had independent information platforms, with proprietary systems for data collection and independent applications for system control. The equivalent would be using one operating system on a computer for writing a text, a different one for drawing, and yet another for listening to music, and where exchanging information between applications would be nearly impossible. They are vertical systems. Fortunately, present-day computing is based on the separation bewteen information capture systems (keyboard, cameras, microphones, etc.), operating systems, and the applications that allow for manipulating information and producing content. And that is where cities will face a great challenge in coming years.

The question is whether each city will have its own urban operating system, the City OS, or if cities and industry will work together to define the standards for managing urban information, so that all cities can have similar, open structures for information management, which will allow for any urban element to be integrated into the city in that same way that an application can be installed on different computers that use the same operating system.

The process of building a city and making it work is not straightforward. Cities, with their functional diversity and their structural complexity, are the most complex systems that humans have created on the Earth. Cities are managed through operative protocols that act on all aspects of urban life and define mechanisms for resilience in the face of exceptional situations. The information society adds a new level of information to the city, which allows for evaluating its operation in real time and, in some cases, predicting potential risks in order to prevent them.

In addition, politics —the art of organizing the polis— is the biggest
generator of urban protocols. Cities are organized according
to rules of social interaction that are defined by the inhabitants
themselves through regulated processes. The construction of a
city supposes a cohabitation pact that sets in stone the spatial
relationships that are established between people, organizations
and businesses to carry out the functions associated with
habitation. The density of cities in Europe or Asia and the
dispersion of American cities isn't just the result of different
technologies having to do with mobility. It is an inherent part of
each culture, in which the ideas of individuality and collectivity
have different meanings. That is why, in each case, different urban,
social or economic protocols are defined to build cities and make
them work.
Every city has laws that are part of the set of government
regulations determined by each country, which are developed in
a particular economic framework and which promote more or less
leadership of public or private structures.
Information networks have led to changes in systems of
government in a number of countries in the world because they
connect people and provide them with the possibility to exert a
directly influence on the politics in their surroundings.
The government systems what will emerge as a result of the
Internet have yet to be seen. New technologies should allow for the
development of mechanisms for more continuous participation in
decision making having to do with urban life. Again, the so-called
information society should develop mechanisms for transmitting
information to society in a transparent way, so that it can be
interpretation for the purpose of decision making, both by city
governments and by citizens.

LINES OF URBAN CODE

Therefore, the anatomy of the city can be organized according to its structure, (environment, infrastructures and built domain), information and people; it can resemble a network.

Let's imagine that we're drawing a graph. On the x-axis, we include every urban function, with as much detail as you like, using a basic division into residences, work places, facilities and infrastructure nodes. On the y-axis, let's imagine there are different scales, from the individual scale of objects all the way up to the planetary scale, as we described it earlier. We should be able to plot any object and building in the world on this graph, because it responds to a concrete function, which can be used by a precise number of people. The third dimension of the graph would bring together all of the nodes that fulfill the same function on the same scale, regardless of their geographic location.

Any human action that needs to be carried out will activate one or more nodes and the infrastructural connections that exist between them, such that there will be jumps in scale from one node to the next. The production of food is one of the vectors of self-sufficiency. Let's imagine that we want to transport a tomato from the place where it was grown to an individual refrigerator. It can be done in a number of ways. If the tomato is produced on a large farm in Brazil, that produces food for hundreds of thousands of people, a local logistics network will transport the tomato by truck to a port, where millions of tons of agricultural production will pass through, to supply millions of people. Then it will be transported on a ship that carries food for thousands of people and it will arrive at a port that receives goods for millions of people. From the port, it will be taken to a central market that serves hundreds of thousands of people; from there it will be transported to a market that takes in goods for

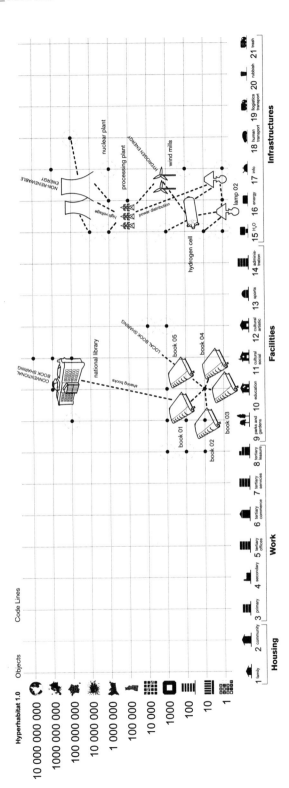

Hyperhabitat: A multiscalar matrix that contains all of the things, buildings and cities on the planet, organized as nodes which enable people to carry out functions.

thousands of people. There, it will finally be sold in a local shop that serves hundreds of people, one of whom will take it back to their individual refrigerator. A serious odyssey.

A less costly version of this process, from an energetic point of view, is a regional farmer who produces food for hundreds of people. When he collects the goods, he fills up his van that can hold food for hundreds of people, transports the tomato to a market that sells goods for thousands of people, where someone buys it and takes it to their individual refrigerator.

A smaller-scale case is also possible, in the case of someone who grows tomatoes in an urban garden in front of his or her house and who picks one, when it's ripe, and takes it directly to the refrigerator, or dinner plate.

The ultimate result is the same: someone has a tomato in the fridge, but the social, environmental and economic impact of the process is completely different. Each of these configurations requires a different way of organizing the territory and urban space.

A chair may be made in China (a scale of one to one million), in a factory that manufactures chairs for a million people, or in a production laboratory located on the ground floor of a nearby building, where each individual can produce his or her own chair (a scale of one to one hundred).

Each jump from one node to the next involves one or more networks that generate a line of code indicating a functional relationship.

Energy can be produced in a nuclear power plant in a neighboring country (a scale of one to ten million), or on the roof of the building where we life (a scale of one to one hundred).

Any decision concerning how human activities, and the associated spaces, are organized implies a different quality of life, and a

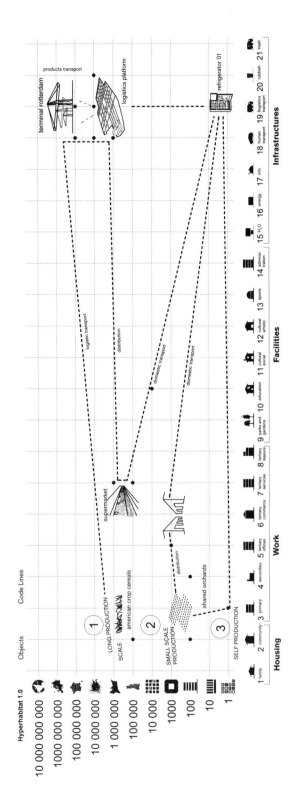

Hyperhabitat, reprogramming the world: three ways of putting food in the refrigerator with the participation of different nodes: global, regional and local.

different cost/benefit ratio. In any case, the idea is not that every citizen should do everything for him or herself, literally. The idea is to use the potential inherent in the local production of resources, based on knowledge that emerges from information networks, so that the production processes and the experiences associated with the production of resources serve to create a more united society. The regeneration of cities based on the model of networked self-sufficiency only makes sense if it allows people to exert more control over their own lives and if it gives them more power, as part of a social network.

REPROGRAMMING THE WORLD

How can we reprogram the world based on the model of a networked habitat?

Industrial society has operated in such a way that the lines of code have flowed from larger-scale structures (resource production centers from the industrial era, always ready to supply energy, water, food or products to millions of people) to smaller-scale structures, composed of individuals. It is in accordance with this logic that cities have been built in recent decades. The information society, in contrast, connects people with people, objects with other objects, buildings with buildings, communities with other communities, so that the flow of resources happens between smaller-scale nodes, which allows for the "emergence" of the system, based on the interaction of thousands nodes with similar characteristics.

If each node that exists on the planet, whatever its scale may be, has a digital identity and the ability to manage information, everything can be connected to everything else.

Reprogramming the world means rewriting the lines of code for

the actions we carry out each day, so that they can happen more
efficiently, using fewer resources, managing more information.
And promoting more social unity.
This programming is carried out by people, companies,
organizations and governments in accordance with the rules for
managing each territory.
In this way, the flows of resources will evolve from the current
model —which connects the large-scale production nodes, which
operate on a scale of one to 1,000,000 or 10,000,000 and serve the
consumer nodes at the scale of 100, 10 or 1— toward models where
small-scale nodes: 1, 10, 100, 1,000, or 10,000, produce and consume
the resources that they share with other similar nodes.
The information necessary for the production of resources will
move across information networks, and it will be shared or sold.
In order to do this, the territories inhabited by Man will have
to be restructure based on new Humanist principles, using the
technological and cultural potential of our time.
It is the "Internet of everything". If the distributed model of the
Internet is applied to reduce the scale at which we carry out our
daily activities, applied in areas like energy, water management,
manufacturing or health services, cities will need to be modified so
that they can function based on new principles.
Architecture, and the organization of human habitats, in this
context, are relevant disciplines for the development of this
regeneration in our physical surroundings, to allow for new forms
of economic and social interaction.

Metropolises, cities, neighborhoods, public space, city blocks,
buildings and homes.
The connected self-sufficient city.

THE SELF SUFFICIENT CITY

1. Dwelling
(1-10)

How does the information society transform living conditions in the area of citizen's private lives? What new operations can housing perform in a networked society?

A dwelling is the central piece in a person's habitability. It is a right of all people. It is, as Marshall McLuhan[5] referred to it, an extension of the skin.

Internet has changed people's ability to interact from within the private sphere and, as a result, on a global scale.

Whereas traditional doctrine stated that a city is a place where people live, work and rest, a place for commerce and a meeting place, as a result of new technologies a person's home can potentially admit all of those functions. We have already mentioned this. The dwelling incorporates the individual-scale nodes from a number of networks that exist in the city. It contains the nerve endings in the city's nervous system.

In the 20th century, we witnessed a process of the "objectification" of functions. Many activities that used to require a specific space and an infrastructure can now be accomplished using a machine. Public laundry sinks in the town squares, and the social activities that took place around them, have disappeared with the advent of the washing machine, which can be found in most homes. Treadmills have taken the place of races through the fields. Computers have substituted, at least partially, dozens of activities that are tied in with physical space, by effecting those activities virtually. And, at the same time, objects have become much smaller.

THE MEDIA HOUSE PROJECT [6]

In 2001, the first year of the Master's Degree in Advanced Architecture, we developed the Media House Project with The Center for Bits and Atoms at MIT. That was when we began working with Neil Gershenfeld [7], the director of "Things That Think" at the Media Lab, maybe the most important center for digital technology at the time.

Our idea was to develop a prototype for an informational dwelling, combining the power of American culture –focused on the objects and the technologies that can be developed generally in a number of different designs– and European culture, more oriented toward questions of space, and capable of combining public and private resources toward an experiment about the future of dwelling.

In the same way that access to electricity and potable water transformed the physical space of dwellings with new spaces and functions at the beginning of the 20th century, the aim was to investigate what kind of functional or spatial changes might be associated with new information technologies.

Neil suggested using a technology developed by his center based on the smallest IP servers in the world. Whereas in the nineteen seventies, an Internet server occupied an entire room and cost millions of dollars, servers could now be manufactured in the size of a dollar coin.

The idea was to provide a dwelling with intelligence based on the creation of a network of microservers embedded in household objects to create a distributed computation system. The dwellings' intelligence was not meant to reside in any of its objects in particular; rather it was to emerge from the relationship between all of its parts. The project stipulated that if every element in the dwelling had a digital identity, everything could be connected to everything else through the buildings network, in a non-centralized way. As such, the building network should be built at the same time as its physical structure.

In the nineteen twenties, with the development of concrete structures, the form of buildings became separate from its structure and the concept of an open plan was developed. The different mechanical systems in buildings were hidden behind drop ceilings and other elements that allowed for organizing the building in layers installed by different specialists.

However, in natural systems, which respond to the optimization of energy consumption, the form and the structure of living beings follow the same logic. And in most cases, they coincide in a single element.

Antoni Gaudí's architecture has often been used to exemplify buildings where the form emerges directly from the forces that serve shape it, and where the different functional systems are integrated into a single constructive element.

In our project, we proposed manufacturing a spatial network using rods that served to define the physical structure of the building, with the energetic structure and the logical structure embedded in a single tube-shaped element. Any electrical element could be connected or disconnected from the network transparently, and the system would recognized the addition of a new element, adapting its configuration to allow for interaction. As such, there is no one element that controls the rest of the dwelling; rather, the intelligence emerges from the interaction of dozens of small elements with minimum intelligence.

Marvin Minsky[8], one of the fathers of artificial intelligence, asserted in his book *The Society of Mind* that he was astonished how the relationship between millions of unintelligent elements (neurons) could generate intelligence. Our approach was similar. And it was completely different from the centralized "domotics" system that are still used in some buildings. In those systems, the intelligence of the building is managed from a central computer through which decisions are made that a range of mechanisms carryout, such that if the central computer fails, the whole building "freezes".

If we wanted to provide objects with intelligence so that we could measure values associated with them (using sensors) in order to manipulate them (with actuators), we needed to know what categories of things exist in the physical confines of a habitable space. And we needed that information in order to decide which parameters should be measured and manipulated. The control of air cycles in office buildings is an illustrative example: at present we are able to know the temperature and the humidity content of the air inside a space (using sensors) and we can manipulate air conditions using air jets (actuators) that release pre-treated air in order to guarantee (if all goes well) constant temperatures and humidity levels according to the user's desires.

We arrived at the conclusion that if we divide the interior space of a dwelling into cubic millimeters and we look at what each of them contains, we only find six categories of elements of different natures: living beings, objects, space, networks, limits and content. Each of these categories can be measured using different parameters, and if we want to alter their behavior, different actuators needed to be defined.

Obviously, in order to be able to establish relationships or algorithms for their behavior, we should to start understand what intelligence is, how many kinds of intelligence we can establish in a space and what type of social, emotional or economic relationships occur when we manipulate elements in the dwelling.

The project was presented in September of 2001 at the Mercat de les Flors in Barcelona as the beginning of a work in progress that was developed in subsequent years.

Throughout the course of the project, we created a spatial structure where objects could be connected and their positions could be freely change, while maintaining the logical relationships with other objects using the embedded microservers. That allowed for experiencing a habitable space with some of the characteristics of digital systems, where everything is reprogrammable, as opposed to traditional dwellings, where the functions and the positions of objects in space are fixed, and they are tied in with the electrical systems that supply them.

We built a house that was controlled by a distributed computer. The Media House was built according to the principle, "The house is the computer. Its structure is the network."

THE COMPUTERS DISSOLVE INTO THE DWELLING.

Beyond the structure, we also experimented with new spaces and functions in dwellings.

Imitating the telegraph rooms found in houses at the beginning of the twentieth century, we developed a specific space reserved for telecommunications, which we called the "croma room", containing a camera for videoconferences and a blue screen where any background for the conversation could be projected.

We also included spaces for children to write on the walls and manipulate the space without the traditional order of conventional houses, where drawing on the walls is not allowed. A space with the capacity to record drawings and images and to store the memory of events. The bedroom was transformed into a space for luminotherapy, where the color of the lights could be adjusted depending on people's moods. A group of students directed by the artist Nuria Díaz created the interface for interacting with the dwelling and the different media systems it incorporated.

The bathroom was a small-scale laboratory where beauty and medicine came together. The kitchen, with its hydroponic garden, was a place where food could be produced and transformed based on shared knowledge. The working Ares, a place dedicated to the production of knowledge and the interaction with other people. In our project, we also experimented with the process of erasing the presence of computers from the dwelling. With distributed computing, we witnessed a process in which computers, became tiny little things that were inset into every element of the dwelling. And screens, which had lower production costs and were produced using flat systems, became larger. In the new dwellings, computers disappear and content takes on the scale of the space.

The project was also an event designed for providing social exposure to the innovations and proposals. The architect Enric Ruiz-Geli designed a performance that condensed a day's activity into an hour so that visitors could see the house in operation and inhabited by a number of different creators.

INTERNET 0. THE INTERNET OF THINGS

The name *Internet 0* was used in that project to refer to the network created by the microservers embedded in the objects in the dwelling. One of the partners in the project was the I2Cat consortium, founded by the engineer Sebastià Sallent and the anthropologist Artur Serra, among others. The aim of the group is to promote high-speed Internet services, such as high definition interactive video, and their introduction on all scales of society. The Media House was also fitted with an Internet 2 network.

At lunch on the day of the opening, Artur asked Neil how fast the data travelled using tiny microservers. The aim of his question was to bring up the current speed of networks, in a debate about the use of high-speed networks. In response to Artur's insistence, Neil introduced the argument that the connection between a light switch and a lamp, or between a thermostat and a watering system in a house, didn't require sending video signals, which do need a lot of bandwidth. What they do need is to be permanently connected and to respond to signals sent out by other sensors and resources. "If you are Internet 2, we'll be Internet 0," Neil finally asserted. In the end, his definition turned out to be brilliant, and it became the name for a line of research at MIT, currently working with a number of international partners. Internet 0 (I0) proposes that, in parallel to the Internet that many people use today via ADSL or fiber optic networks, there should be another very low-speed Internet capable of connecting objects with one another.

An Internet that connects trillions of elements that simply change their status from on to off, measure elemental data from reality and communicate it to neighboring elements, provide information on their position and their availability, and change the status of actuators.

In the wake of commercial Internet and social Internet, the Internet of things emerges based on technologies like Internet 0.

In order for this vision to be developed, it is not enough to create sensors and actuators that send data to a centralized computer that controls the different parts of a dwelling or a city. The algorithms for controlling the system should be distributed throughout the system, so that if one part of the system crashes, the rest can continue operating normally.

The logical capacity of a system should increase as its physical structure increases. The "killer application" of the Internet of things, the one that leads a solution to develop on a global level, will be energy networks in buildings and energy efficiency in cities.

THE INTERNET OF ENERGY
Ten years later at the IAAC we started the Energrid project in the context of the Novare prizes, organized by the largest energy company in Spain, Endesa. The aim of the project was to develop "the Internet of energy" based on managing the information on elements that generate and consume energy in dwellings, buildings, neighborhoods and cities.

In fact, the largest electricity companies, which supply energy to buildings from large production centers (at a scale of 1 to 1,000,000), have very little information on internal electrical consumption because meters are always installed on the dividing line between the exterior and the interior of the dwelling. The same thing happens with water. If the energy savings for thousands of dwellings can be managed simultaneously, or if peaks in consumption can be predicted, or if the activation of specific elements in the dwelling can be limited (with a certain level of economic compensation), it will improve energy management in cities, because it will allow for limiting consumption peaks at specific points in time. It's what is called the "long tail", where the aggregation of a large number of microconsumption points can decisively affect the management of a large network.

In fact, in coming years, the price of energy will depend on its source and the distance between generation and consumption. In this way, different prices could be applied for consumption associated with different household appliances with respect to the time of day, with the fundamental aim of reducing peaks in

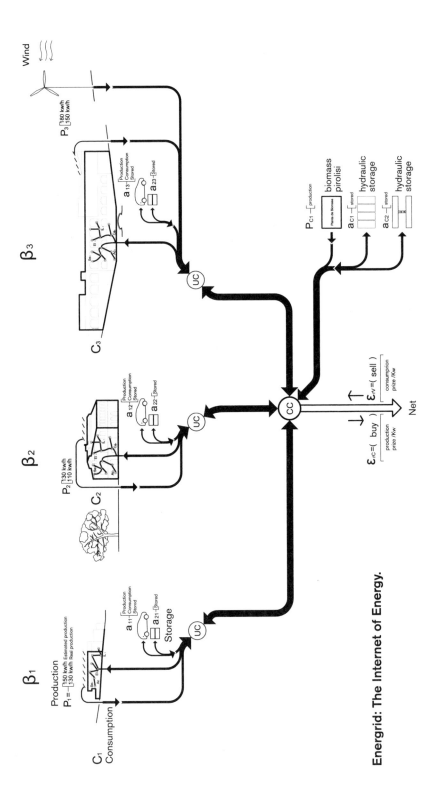

Energrid: The Internet of Energy.

demand. The energy will emit signals containing information on its price. As such, possessing active information on each of the nodes that generate and consume resources will allow for making decisions about each consumption point individually, as opposed to referencing the dwelling as a whole, as is currently the case. This will increase the degree of resolution of electrical energy consumption and it will allow for more precise management of the entire system.

The Energrid network will differentiate consumption points (any electrical element), from consumption units (associated with the old meters for each dwelling) and consumption communities, which will allow for the creation of a local energy micronetwork. If a number of different dwellings or buildings can generate energy locally, then each dwelling should decide whether to consume it, store it (in an electric vehicle or in batteries) or sell it to the community or the network based on principles that will have been programmed beforehand.

At the IAAC, in the Fab Labs network and at the UPC, we have been working on the design of a low-cost network of small inset computers that can be manufactured locally, with the aim of implementing a personalized network of sensors, using different standards of open code, such as Ardunio or Internet 0 itself.

REPROGRAMMING THE WORLD

In 2008, we were invited to participate in the 11th International Architecture Exhibition at the Venice Biennale of Architecture, titled "Architecture Beyond Building"[2] and curated by Aaron Betsky. For the exhibition, we built an installation using the Hyperhabitat principle, where different objects in the dwelling, built to represent x-rays of themselves, are fitted with a small

Internet 0 server and a slider switch that changes the scale of the selected functional category. By way of a small sensor, links can be established between the objects and their associated scales. These links can be viewed in a large-scale projection created by the company Bestiario, which also displays the relationships between nodes at different scales in a hypothetical city.

With this project we imagine that, in the near future, every object and every building in the world will have a digital identity. And citizens will be able to register their physical belongings on the network in order to create communities of people who can share resources (books, tools, etcetera). And, in the best case scenario, organization located in the same city will be able to share auditoriums or meeting rooms that habitually go unused. In fact, every city, every territory could have its own Hyperhabitat map linked to the objects and buildings in it, in order to stimulate the creation of new lines of code to define the functional relationships between one thing and another.

Whereas up to the present the economy has been based on buying and selling products, with the right information, different relationships associated with the interchange of goods can be created. Objects can be bought, sold, shared, loaned out or given away. All of these situations are characteristic of communities where there is more social interaction, and shopping centers aren't the only meeting places. In times of crisis, in cities where there are compact communities, there are a number of different phenomena associated with time banks, where people exchange work hours that are associated with a value.

In the same way that the creators of Google decided that they wanted to "download" the Internet onto their computers (and they managed), we would like to "upload" the physical world onto the Internet.

It would be a way of stimulating the capacities of people would possess or manage nodes, from a hotel to a gymnasium; from a biomass power plants to a small water treatment plant; from a kitchen to neighborhood school, etc. in order to create new types of functional interactions in cities. This promotes social interaction which, in turn, promotes mutual reinforcement of the people and the organizations that inhabit a territory.

THE MATERIAL HISTORY OF OBJECTS

Every object on the planet has a material history and a formal genealogy.

All objects are physically different from one another. Each particular object was made at a particular time, which a specific material, by a particular organization or person, based on a specific design. That production process had a social, environmental and economic impact on a certain area of the planet. With globalization, we have lost the trail of where the objects that we use every day come from, how they were made and who made them. Food has a similar history.

The timber industry has created a label, the FSC, to evaluate the environmental impact of its production and assess whether it is parts of a cycle that could be referred to as sustainable. However, beyond the use of a more general label, each piece of wood furniture should be associated with the geographic location of the tree from which it was made, where it was manipulated, who produced the object, how it was transported and, as the case may be, who its owners have been.

In many cases, objects evolve based on other objects; sometimes they are created by specific designers, and sometimes they are the product of a business culture or a local culture.

In a "knowledge city," we should be able to access all of the information associated with any of the objects in our surroundings. This information lets us know whether, above and beyond the price of things, we might recognize the values associated with an object as our own.

Objects should guarantee that they are part of a natural cycle. That they come from nature and that they will return to nature when they are recycled and transformed into other objects, or that they can decompose into nature.

If we follow the logic of a planet understood as a Hyperhabitat, objects should have a digital identity produced at a very low cost, with an IP address that allows them to connect with other objects in their surroundings. Every object should be fitted with an identification system. Based on that system, we should be able to access each object's personal web information, in a kind of Wikipedia of objects, the Objectpedia, that compiles the material history and the genealogy of every functional node on the planet.

DWELLINGS TO PROMOTE QUALITY IN CITIES

Dwellings can connect people, instead of keeping them apart. More and more personal nodes connect with other nodes every day, through information networks and especially social media, to share resources and information.

All the same, we write dozens of emails any number of people and we "friend" other on Facebook whom we have never even met Howe can the Internet be used as a mechanism for promoting local interaction and creating communities? Creating a community, feeling identified with your home and your neighborhood is key to bringing meaning back to the city, making it more habitable, more secure.

Jerilyne Perine, the former director of the public housing authority in New York, the Housing Preservation and Development Department (HPD), participated, in 2007, in a workshop on housing for the Master's degree in Advanced Architecture. She told us about how the public housing authority for New York was created in the nineteen seventies, during a period of high inflation and an energy crisis. The goal was to build and manage accessible housing with the aim of establishing the population in the city to help them identify with a place. She asserted that if the question of access to a house at a reasonable price is resolved (to own or to rent), citizens can think about setting up business, having families, such that human relationships are consolidated in the territory, making cities more secure and united.

This policy of building housing for social groups in need has been a big success in New York and it still serves as a tool for regenerating deteriorated areas.

Housing has often been seen as another way of investing savings. For many year, it has been defines as one more product. Houses need to be bought because they're made to be bought! Banks also helped in the process. Over the past few years, house size in Spain has depended on the relationship between the price of land and the amount of money that banks could lend, based on a person's income.

Housing seen as a commodity from the seller's point of view. Habitability should be dealt with like mobility. The automobile is one format of private mobility, nearly the only one that citizens can buy. There are other formats, however (trains, buses, airplanes, shared bikes) that can be used for mobility, which don't have to be purchased.

Surely, something similar could be done with housing. We should promote building for rent, shared housing, single-generation or multi-generation residences, hotels for scientists, residences for travelers. Each one promotes a different relationship between the different parts and functions of a dwelling.

Historically, housing has been associated with "hearths" or fireplaces. Like an ancestral ritual. Throughout history, housing has established physical limits to sensorially divide the different functions that various individuals can carry out, limiting sight, hearing and smell. Current housing follows functional parameters designed by the Bauhaus school in the nineteen twenties, in which a definition was provided for what a kitchen and a bathroom would look like in the 20th century, and the minimum dimensions were established.

What fundamental functions, then, should be included in housing for the 21st century? In 2002, we undertook research at the IAAC to try to understand what constitutes a dwelling and to determine its essential elements. Is your home is where you have your bed, your wardrobe, or your kitchen?

Every dwelling should allow for carrying out at least thirteen functions associated with objects, which are:

Sleep - bed
Storage - closet
Washing - shower
Defecating - toilet
Cleaning - sink
Cooking - kitchen
Eating - table
Rest - armchair
Communication - computer
Laundry - washing machine
Conservation - refrigerator

Other functions like exercise, study or shopping are not associated
with housing; they correspond to neighborhoods.

Nearly any place where a person can sleep in a Western city allows
for carrying out all of those functions. But it is their organization,
their degree of individuality and their management systems, that
differentiates a dwelling from a hotel, a rest home from a reform
school or a prison.

Mark Wigley, the dean of Columbia University's Graduate School
of Architecture, Planning and Preservation told me about the
Million Dollar Blocks[9] project which mapped the geographic
origins of people who had been found guilty of crimes in the
United States. They discovered that the federal government had left
off building social housing and had begun using the funds that had
historically been invested in housing to build prisons. A different
kind of lodging. The conclusion was that if a million dollars had
been invested in educational and social infrastructures in the city
blocks where the majority of prison residents grew up, it could have
prevented their ending up in prison in the first place.

Living doesn't mean buying a house. It means organizing the
development of human beings as individuals and as a collective
through the sequence of functions that are carried out at different
frequencies.

But urban design has forgotten its condition as a generator of
habitability and interaction, and it has become a mechanism for
managing the benefits and burdens of the transformation of urban
land. An informational urban design focused on improving human
habitability should promote more interaction between inhabitants
and the activities that turn them into members of a community.
In order for that to be possible, the networks associated with
human habitability need to be included among their competencies.

Today, cities are designed with the assumption that electricity will be brought in from somewhere else. Either from a nuclear power plant in a neighboring country, or an underwater gas pipe from a country that isn't interested in transforming that natural wealth into economic and social progress for its inhabitants.

In the same way that the city guarantees mobility through physical public space, it should also guarantee universal access to information networks, in addition to building mechanisms for collective interaction. The public sector has remained entirely passive before the cultural change represented by the information society. Public organizations have been passive consumers (just like any individual or company) of the content structured by big businesses through the Internet.

Housing, like a microcity, should allow for carrying out all of the functions that can be undertaken by the administration. But the network is not just a new, more efficient way of doing the same old things The surrounding conditions can change if we are able to heighten our ability to manage the information contained in dwellings, which could be shared.

MACROAPARTMENTS WITH SHARED SPACES

Housing regulations are outdated in many Western countries. They were developed for very large dwellings, where many people would live together. Today, the family unit is different. 21% of households in Spain are made up of people living alone. A loft, an empty space with one enclosed volume for a bathroom, would be considered an illegal space.

Sharing housing resources with other units nearby, as a result of sharing information about the available resources, is an excellent way of increasing our efficiency, sometimes avoiding the

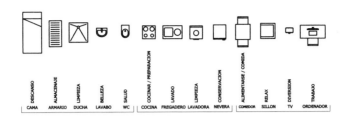

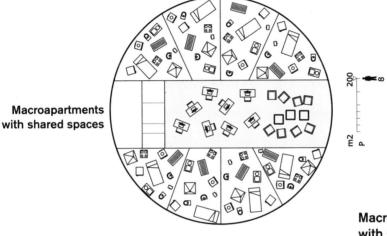

**Macroapartments
with shared spaces**

**Macroapartments
with shared spaces
versus
Miniapartments.**

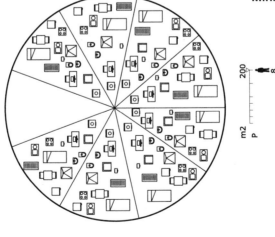

Miniapartments

consumption of public resources, and increasing social cohesion. This is precisely one of the paradigms of the Internet. Music, videos, text and other digital resources are an important application of the network. Napster changed the history of music because it demonstrated that it could be organized according to different rules, beyond buying and selling albums.

In 2002 we developed the *Sharing Tower* project, in the framework of "Sociopolis"[10], which made its first appearance at the Valencia Biennale in 2003. The idea was that, in the same way other resources can be shared, physical space can also be shared to do "more with less".

During the 1920s in the Soviet Union, buildings were put up like the Narkomfin building, designed by Moisei Ginzburg in 1928, where the kitchen was communal. The socialist idea of deconstructing the traditional family structure was represented by spaces where people could cook and eat their meals with the whole community, in groups of a hundred people.

It is impossible to share a kitchen with a hundred people. At most, it would be a public kitchen, like in a restaurant or a hotel, or even on a military base. It has to be governed by something that extends beyond the relationships between one individual and another. With the *Sharing Tower*, we understood that physical resources could be shared in groups of four, eight or up to a maximum of sixteen people. A shared space emerges from the voluntary connection between potentially private spaces, and individual activities. We discovered, in short, that the number of people sharing a physical resource is fundamental to defining its meaning.

Dozens of students share apartments in cities. And it's illegal, as everyone knows, because (in general) it implies paying someone – the person who rents the apartment– under the table. In Barcelona, three or four-bedroom apartments in the Eixample are often shared by groups of students. What is unbelievable is that no one ever designs apartments that are meant to be shared, despite the fact that young people often do it, because it represents a very efficient solution.

Our *Sharing Tower* emerged with the idea that, instead of designing miniapartments of 45m² (the minimum under Spanish law), where each young person would have all of the necessary resources for a dwelling, we could create shared "macro-apartments" where each inhabitant would have some private resources and others that he or she would share in spaces designed for that purpose. To my surprise, the new Housing Plan for 2003 included a provision that allowed for building mini-apartments that could share 20% of their surface area with other units. The surface area in question was intended for use as a laundry room, or similar facilities, on each floor.

In our project, we proposed organizing each floor with a different configuration of relationships among the apartments. Resources would be shared in groups of two, four or eight, which allowed for creating a shared kitchen, living room, or office for a fixed micro-community of people. The design was for a shared macro-apartment, as opposed to micro-apartments.

We used the new law to develop the *Sharing Tower* on a specific site in the La Torre neighborhood of Valencia, in the framework of the Sociopolis project. The project was selected by Terence Riley, curator of Architecture and Design at the Museum of Modern Art in New York (MoMA), for the exhibition "On Site"[11] on Spanish architecture in 2006. "I would have liked to live in that building," Terry said. And, at nearly the same time, I met Ramón Ruiz, an innovative entrepreneur who had come to the same conclusion about building

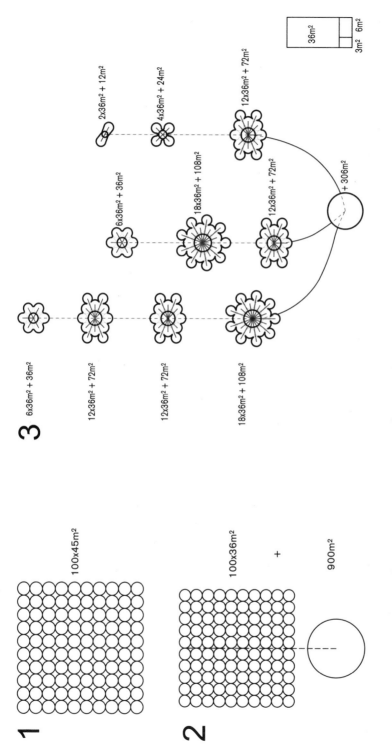

Shared Blocks in Gandia (Valencia)
On how to organize 100 dwellings: all of the private spaces, private and shared spaces, and private spaces with two scales of shared spaces.

1   100x45m²

2   100x36m²   +   900m²

3   6x36m² + 36m²

     12x36m² + 72m²

     12x36m² + 72m²

     18x36m² + 108m²

6x36m² + 36m²

18x36m² + 108m²

12x36m² + 72m²

2x36m² + 12m²

4x36m² + 24m²

12x36m² + 72m²

+ 306m²

36m²

3m²   6m²

social housing rental units on land reserved for public use, a model that could be applied to housing for young university students. Another example of how technology can connect discontinuous physical entities, to create entities of an order greater than the sum of their parts, is the idea of the discontinuous hotel. In Venice, Paris, Barcelona and other cities in the world, there are a large number of websites offering short-term apartment rentals which, for the most part, are in a situation of alegality. The function of the hotel –gathering together a series of spaces to spend a night– is carried out by the website itself. Instead of taking an elevator to get from one room to the next, you might have to take a taxi.

TELEWORK

Dwellings as workplaces is another of the major paradigms of the information society. In *The End of Work*[12], Jeremy Rifkin already announced that, in the information society, the people who do work will work a lot On the other hand, there will be a lot of people without work. Knowledge workers will always have work, connected to the network. As such, in many cases, people's houses will also be their workplaces. It always has been for many people, like freelancers. But now, parents and children will share spaces, resources, printers and bandwidth because we will continue working, even after we arrive home. Sometimes with more independence and pleasure, because it will beyond the reach of phone calls and meetings.

The concept of homes as workplaces has moved beyond the format for teleworking that was developed at the end of the 1990s, where people stayed at home to work instead of going into the office. Today, teleworkers work on trains and in cafés, as well as at home.

PERSONAL MANUFACTURING

A large amount of the functional and energetic efficiency that we expect to help transform cities comes from the ability to access more information about reality, and to connect it with other similar realities in other systems, both in public space and the private space of the home. Of the three basic elements to be produced in a city –energy, food and goods (obviously together with the knowledge needed to manage them)–, in the coming years, dwellings will come to house different systems which will allow for the production of goods through digital manufacturing.

Personal computers and printers have made it possible for people's houses to become working spaces. Next in the series comes the personal manufacturing device, associated with 3D printers that are able to produce any object using high-density resins or other materials that may be developed in the near future.

The exhibition on digital manufacturing, *Full Print3d*, put together at the Dhub in Barcelona in 2010, curated by Marta Malé-Alemany, one of the foremost international experts in digital manufacturing, and coordinated by Areti Markopoulou, demonstrated that the production of objects no longer has to be associated with industrial systems that produce thousands of identical pieces using repetitive processes. The new digital printers are the equivalent of the personal printers that can be found in any home in industrialized countries, except they can print objects. These machines, which today are still rare, will be the equivalent of washing machines in the 1960s, that transformed how homes were organized and made domestic tasks much less time-consuming.

In fact, work is currently being done on machines that manufacture machines, that is to say that they have the ability to replicate themselves so that even the production of the machines themselves can take place locally. In a world where the production many of objects that are used in daily life can happen in our homes or where the production of objects in our buildings, or our city blocks, can take place in a copy shop, the rules of industrial production are completely changed.

This technology can signify a paradigm shift similar to when the printing press was invented, or the steam engine, in that it individualizes the production of objects, and gives the dwelling back the productive character it had in medieval cities, or in the California garages where the computer culture was first born.

As such, the dwelling is transformed into a microcity, where people can work, rest and produce energy, while they are connect to their local and global surroundings via information networks. The dwelling and its architecture can stimulate people's creativity. If dwellings in medieval warrior society took the shape of castles and walled cities, what will dwellings look like in the information society?

2. Building
(100)

How do the distributed systems that are characteristic of the
Internet affect the design and construction of buildings? How can
buildings be designed to act as active organisms within urban
ecosystems? Can buildings be self-sufficient?
Human beings wouldn't need houses or cities if they were
interested in living naked out in the middle of nature.
Our ancestors did it.
A building is a habitable structure, the fundamental mission of
which is to create stable boundary conditions for human activities.
Buildings emerged as a part of the logic of setting up stable
settlements in the territory, associated with the production of food,
goods and energy, and with community living.
The history of civilizations is manifested through the history of
their buildings. Each civilization is associated with a different
degree of knowledge in the manipulation of natural resources to
produce materials for their construction. Buildings are designed
and constructed using each society's own technology and culture.
Greek temples, the domes of Persian markets or Renaissance
churches in Rome are all manifestations of the depth of the human
spirit, which comes to life, timelessly, in certain places on Earth, at
certain moments in history, as the expression of a civilization.
Buildings are the basic unit of an architectural project. Architecture
is the art of dwelling.
Buildings are part of the material cycle of the world. Their materials
come from nature and will return to nature as debris. Where
industrialization allow for the development of manufactured
materials, like steel or concrete, and later plastic petroleum-based

products, now we are working toward the development of materials that do not contain chemical elements which, when they return to nature, are sources of pollution.

Buildings, as functional nodes in the multiscalar habitat in which we live, must be transformed into producers of resources, as opposed to mere consumers. They need to incorporate new systems and technologies which will change them into active entities in the interchange of the city's energy and information.

Whereas, in the 20th century, the physical structure of buildings was transformed, moving from load-bearing walls to reticulated structures, in the 21st century buildings will incorporate a metabolism of their own, which will change the way buildings relate to the environment in which they are built.

Buildings, like organisms in urban ecosystems, form an organized and complex material structure , participated in by information systems, and which establishes a relationship with the environment through the exchange of material and energy in an orderly fashion, and which has the ability to perform the basic functions of dwelling. Architecture, according to the biologist Ramon Folch, is a particular case of ecology, in the same way that medicine relates to zoology.

SELF-SUFFICIENT BUILDINGS

In the year 2005, we looked on, with astonishment, as housing prices continued to soar while the objective value failed to increase. The value of nearly any good does down over time and with use: a vehicle, a computer... And yet, the prices of office buildings and apartments kept getting higher. Logically, the illusion blew up, because it was "the market", through multiple agents, that was causing the increase.

In any case, in 2005, we launched an Internet competition at the

IAAC, called *Self-Sufficient Housing*[13], coordinated by the architect Lucas Cappelli. The goal was to create self-sufficient buildings by defining new technological paradigms and integrating them through design. If a building is going to be more expensive, it should do a lot more. And the local generation of energy seemed like a new requirement for buildings.

The result of the initiative was that we received more than fifteen hundred entries from students and architects from a hundred different countries, who sent in different proposals that negotiated with the technological and the formal, the organic and the natural. This initiative gave way to other competitions, like *Self-Fab House*[14] or *Self-Sufficient City*[15], which helped us discover new talents and develop a framework for debate and international research on self-sufficient habitats.

Buildings consume a third of the energy that is consumed worldwide, and of that percentage, 10% corresponds to urban, non-industrial buildings.

In the nineteen twenties, a large number of paradigms were defined for new buildings. There was a moment during the 20th century when the fascination for mechanization and artificial control served to define a model in which buildings were net consumers of resources, especially energy and water, and generators of urban waste material. It was a race to improve people's quality of life, also rooted in the advance of democracy, and there was a tendency toward improving living conditions for the majority of citizens in Europe and America.

Metropolises were structured toward the external production of the energy that was to be consumed internally, and used to centralize and sterilize the management of the waste materials and grey water generated there. It worked up to a certain magnitude, both in physical terms and human terms. Today, in the West, cities are butting up against their neighbors, and many of the elements that were once external have been absorbed into the continuous built magma that surrounds cities.

We are now experiencing an internalization process with respect to cities' infrastructures. Buildings, as physical and legal entities, need to recognize the productive elements that they can take on.

If in the 20th century, the regulations required that all buildings include lighting infrastructures and running water, in the 21st century, the regulations will require that all buildings produce as much energy as they consume.

If we study natural patterns, we see that trees produce the energy they need to live, and they function because they are physically connected to the ground that lets them carry out the biochemical exchanges necessary for their survival.

Buildings should be like trees: self-sufficient organisms rooted in a particular reality.

If in the 20th century there was a change in building paradigms as a result of new physical structures made of steel and concrete, in the 21st century there will be a paradigm shift as a result of new logical and energetic structures.

Housing is no longer a dwelling machine.

Buildings are dwelling organisms.

Buildings can be self-sufficient and they can be connected to other buildings and other networks to define the processes of exchange between production and consumption.

In order for that to be possible, intelligent networks need to be developed to manage buildings generation and consumption processes. We dedicated our efforts toward that end in the Energrid project.

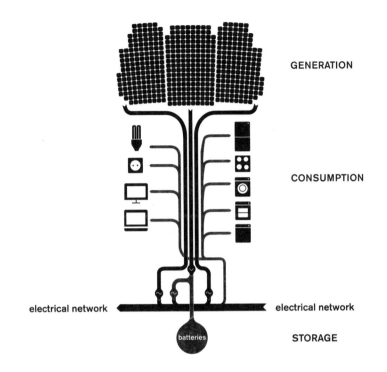

GENERATION

CONSUMPTION

electrical network   electrical network

batteries   STORAGE

A house is like a tree: its roof produces energy, which is sent to batteries where it is stored. Its fruits are light and energy.

THE ELECTRIFICATION OF SOCIETY

In fact, the electrification of society will allow for relating systems that are currently separate (housing, mobility, production) in the same way that digital systems have allowed for the interaction of different media.

A large part of the success of the information society has been due to the digitalization of a number of resources that used to be analog. We listened to music on records, television was broadcast through the air and telephone signals travelled via cable. Books were read, and are still read, on paper. Digital technology has allowed for the creation of new platforms where all of those media are interconnecting and they create synergies. Today, we use electricity for lighting, for home appliances, and in some cases, to heat buildings.

Cars are a separate question. When I was a child, there was an urban legend about an electric car that had been invented, but the inventor had "disappeared" as a result of the interests of oil-producing countries. It was a widely distributed myth. Ten years ago, I saw the first fuel cell car, powered by hydrogen, which seemed like it represented the future of energy sources for the automotive industry. However, ten years later it seems that the industry has developed lithium ion batteries that are more efficient and clean, which are the ones that have been used in the first electric cars that have been produced industrially.

High-speed trains are electric, in contrast to the coal-powered or gas-powered trains of the past. The electrification process seems unstoppable, and it could allow for the creation of synergies between the building industry and urban mobility. As such, buildings, as potential producers of energy, will be essential nodes for the generation of energy in cities, in close proximity to where that energy is consumed.

Automobiles will be the place where the energy produced in buildings can be stored. And the energy in an automobile will be able to power a washing machine or a computer. And a hundred automobiles parked and connected could recharge a city bus. Automobiles will be like the buildings' hard drive, used to store the energy that is produced, as opposed to information.

The automotive industry, which is multinational and global, will interact with the building industry, which is local in many cases, through the common language of energy.

Electrification will be to the physical world what digitalized has been to the information society.

ADDING VALUE TO THE TERRITORY

Real-estate development is used, on a global scale, as a permanent platform for investment or, in most cases speculation.

In the traditional model for the urbanization of the territory, there are two moments in which value is added to a place.

The transformation of rural land into urban land, through urbanization, is the process through which the parameters for the transformation of the territory are defined. Definitions are provided for: density, uses, the type of urbanization, facilities, general systems and other elements that will serve to constitute the city. Through this administrative process, the price of land increases, without necessarily increasing in value. Once land belongs to a new category, it has a different price.

Many large fortunes have been made through this process, in which there is no increase in the material value of a place. Having a purchase option on a plot of land, requalifying it and selling it without even having bought it is common practice in the western world, which is in keeping with the stock market speculation that has been seen in recent years. The territory is like a casino.

Another moment that requires a greater effort is the construction of a building. The aim of anyone in business is to maximize profits. But, when the construction of a building implies a spatial, visual and urban impact for citizens, construction should be an activity tied in with excellence.

After decades of construction along the Mediterranean coastline, future generations will be condemned to suffer the consequences of this short-term economic development.

Whereas in the 19th century, value was added to the territory by transforming agricultural land into urban land, in the 21st century we can add more value to the territory by regenerating cities in order to make them self-sufficient. Making buildings self-sufficient means adding value to currently inert structures.

Building according to current techniques is relatively simple. All buildings have to guarantee structural security and a series of minimum networks. In Spain, when developers urbanize land, they are required to build infrastructures for water, electricity, communications and waste material, which are handed over to the city council to handle the connection of those buildings to the large-scale networks.

In Spain, at the present, all of those infrastructures are managed by private companies. Urbanization implies the transfer of a series of systems to companies, based on certain protocols that lead to a situation of near-monopoly.

This situation does not occur in any other sector. Except the urbanization of the territory.

What is really relevant is that up to now, developers built as cheaply as possible, with as generic a design as possible, in order to encompass as broad a population as possible, and once the product resulting from the urbanization process was sold, they turned their backs on the place.

Build cheap, sell high, and hit the road.

Now, we know that the potential lies in sticking around. Securing a life-long client, who needs to be supplied with electricity, water, heating, telephone services and content, is what most companies that operate those infrastructures aspire to. Just like in the automobile sector, where automobile prices are set with a tight margin in order to allow for managing its maintenance, building maintenance and the provision of resources is a sector of the economy which will need to be promoted in coming years.

In contrast the model of building cheap, selling high and getting out, new developers will want to build well, sell or rent at a fair price, and stick around to manage the provision of services indefinitely.

If we understand the economy of the information society to be focused on producing and selling products, the information society is based on a service economy. Building as service hubs. Cities as centers for dwelling services.

ENERGY SERVICES COMPANIES

That is how energy services companies came about, called ESCo (Energy Service Company).

The business model for these companies is based on the idea of investing a certain amount in buildings so that they can produce energy (through photovoltaic systems, windmills or other) and so they are better isolated, and then creating a control system that allows for improving the buildings operations to make a return on their investment based on the savings that are generated. That could mean the creation of energy services companies for every building, city block or neighborhood.

One fundamental variable for evaluating possible investments and returns is the price of energy and the premiums (as the case may be) for the generation of energy using renewable systems.

However, Spanish law allow for the production of food and products to be sold to neighbors, but it does not permit the production and sale of electricity (or an Internet connection) for resale to neighbors. It is unbelievable that the two key aspects of our culture, energy and information, are regulated in such a way that citizens are not free to produce them and engage in trade with them, like with any other economic activity.

Traditional power is based on the control of a few key questions, like military force, finance, energy or information. The local production of energy and its direct trade and exchange in an unregulated manner would break with the logic of the control of habitats, production and mobility which energy implies.

It is also true that the emergence of systems for the micromanagement of energy requires a new energy culture, both among citizens and among energy companies and cities' own management, and in the infrastructures designed for that purpose. In the case of renewable energies, many countries decided initially that all of the energy produced had to be sold to the network, compensating for this micro-production with quantities far in excess of the price at which it could be repurchased later. If energy is sold, the premiums in existence up to the present make it more profitable to sell it to the network and repurchase it than to make direct use of the energy produced. This situation is sure to change. Eventually, citizens will pay the real price for energy; renewable energies will no longer be subsidized and the cost of production will be equivalent to other technologies.

When that happens, self-sufficient buildings will make all the energetic sense in the world.

In 2009, the City Council of Sant Cugat del Vallès, a town in Barcelona's metropolitan area, Acciona and the IAAC came to an agreement to evaluate the possible development of a self-sufficient building. The initial idea was to be able to literally disconnect from the electric grid, given the obstacles that electricity companies tend to put in the way of developing certain kinds of projects. It is technically possible, but it isn't legally possible yet.

In this project, a public company would finance the housing and the extra investment for the local production of energy would be financed by and energy services company. During fifteen years, then, the energy produced locally by that company would be sold, then the infrastructure would be transferred to the City Council. In theory, the energy production would be carried out using a small biomass plant or through geothermal energy complemented by photovoltaic systems. Finally, instead of being off-grid, we proposed that it should be "zero emissions," i.e., that the annual difference between production and consumption would be equal to zero. Sometimes, zero-emissions buildings are just a politically correct concept, but they imply a certain amount of euphemism. Some buildings claim to be zero-emissions, but they only generate locally 10% of the energy they need, and to compensate for the emissions of greenhouse gases, thousands of trees have to be planted in another location, while the buildings are under construction. Accounting maneuvers, once again.

In Gandia (Valencia), we built a building with the company Visoren (Social Housing for Rent) for young university students. In this case, the company builds and manages housing on public land in a concession for a period of forty year, and they have the possibility of offering other services associated with the rent. In the process, they reached an agreement with Endesa, the company that will provide the energy services by buying gas from a supplier, producing hot water locally to supply to users and producing electricity, the excess of which will be sold to the network.

The building produces a large portion of the energy it needs to operate, but it will obviously not be zero emissions, because its basic energy is derived from natural gas.

In both cases, the model works economically and, as such, could be extended to other locations.

The fact that buildings will produce energy will change the relationship between buildings and automobiles. If a building produces energy, the decision can be made as to whether to consume that energy locally, sell it to the network, store it in batteries in the building itself, or store it in automobiles.

An intelligent management system should be able to assess the price of energy at any moment and decide what each building should do (or each user within a building if the system is segregated) with the energy it produces.

In the case of Barcelona, the city blocks that make up the Eixample include buildings that can create energy production units based on the relationships between a number of owners-generators and consumers, in order to create a more dynamic system. It would be useful to analyze how to reward the communities that produce their own energy and which, as a result, will not depend on large-scale infrastructures outside of cities.

The biggest challenge presented by these new principles that entail the local production of energy, its intelligent management and, optionally, waste material recycling and water treatment, is the development of new designs that integrate all of those aspects will city dwellers' living conditions.

BUILDING PARAMETERS

Current buildings are defined according to their form and their function. They should also be given a metabolism.

If today buildings are defined using parameters that have to do with their height, building depth, their total floor area and the permitted uses, other parameters should be added to emphasize their efficiency.

We should be able to describe a building's anatomy, like an organism's, (its form and its parts), its physiology (its function) and its metabolism (energy flow and systems).

If a building generates all of the energy that is consumed within the building, should the taxes paid on it really be the same as for the surrounding buildings? Self-sufficient buildings reduce a country's energy dependence and eliminate the need for creating large-scale transmission infrastructures to ensure supply. Buildings should have an epsilon coefficient that reflects the relationship between the energy they generate and the energy they consume on an annual basis. A coefficient of one, or more than one, should be rewarded (at least initially) with lower taxes. Similarly, water consumption should be fixed using an alpha coefficient that defines the consumption of water per inhabitant, how much is recycled and the amount of rainwater that can be stored.

The word Barcelona contains the initials of the parameters that buildings should incorporate in order to evaluate their operation, linked to the different networks that run through buildings and cities:

B be good
A aqua
R recycling
C circulation
E energy
L logistics
O_2 air quality
N nature
@ information

As such, buildings should set parameters concerning their metabolism, which should have the same importance as their physical and operational parameters.

The inclusion of values related to the building operations in the transformation of the city can help us leave behind "Barcelona posa't guapa" for "Barcelona, regenerate", where citizens will be active agents in the changes that are effected, not just on the surface, but in functional and energetic structures.

THE SOLAR HOUSE

In summer of 2010, the IAAC participated in the Solar Decathlon competition, with the project *Fab Lab House*[16] organized by the United States government's Energy secretary, the Spanish Ministry of Housing and the Polytechnic University of Madrid. When the competition began in Washington in 2002, launched by Richard King, the idea was to promote the development of solar housing by universities and research centers, with the aim of demonstrating that it was technically possible, and to encourage the creation of consortiums and working groups that would be dedicated to the effort.

Many of the projects that had been presented in previous years were energy efficient, but they often employed solutions that were very elementary from a spatial and formal point of view. A solar house is more than just a house with solar panels on the roof.

We decided to put together an international team, made up of participants in the Self-Sufficient Housing competition and students in the Master's program at the IAAC. Our design was based on the shape that would have the most interior volume and the least surface area: the sphere. From a natural perspective, it is the most efficient because it has the minimum exterior surface area that needs to be insulated.

When we transformed this primitive form to adapt to a specific location, with respect to the exposure to sunlight, it resulted in a ovoid. Then we lifted that surface off the ground to create a two-

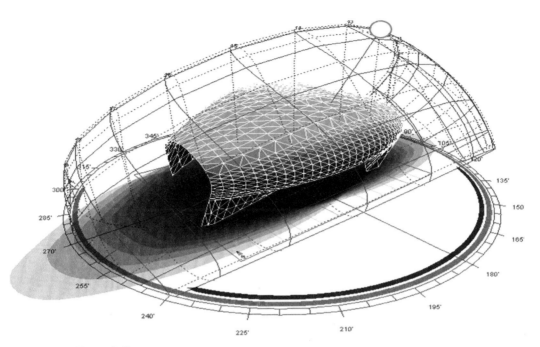

Form follows energy

story building, one in the open air and one enclosed, without any significant increase in the budget. This solution generated a structure that captures sunlight with active systems and produces a large expanse of shade under the house to provide well-being through passive systems, common in Mediterranean architecture. If in the 20th century the saying was "form follows function," now we can assert that "form follows energy".

Nature has always worked that way.

If, for years, software has helped us to draw more efficiently and, recently, to produce different-shaped pieces using numeric manufacturing, new programs allow for evaluating a proposed form with respect to its potential for energy production, and then modifying that form repeatedly until the best solution is found. Buildings should produce energy, but they also need to control energy consumption, both when they are being built and during their service lives.

We decided that the solar house should be produced using a material that had grown due to the effects of the sun: in this case, wood, which is a recyclable material, produced by nature, and which develops as a result of the effects of the atmosphere on the land. Our solar house also took on another challenge involving the inclusion of solar production in the building. We wanted to use a flexible photovoltaic material in order to produced a more naturally curved surface. We tried working with a new generation system based on technology like *copper iridium gallium selenide* (CIGS), but it wasn't available at the time, aside from the fact that its efficiency was only about 10%.

In the end, we improvised. We bought the most efficient solar cells in the world, produced by Sun Power, and with the help of engineer Oscar Aceves, one of the pioneers of photovoltaic systems in Spain, we encapsulated them between layers of Teflon, which is flexible. Thus, we produced what is probably the most efficient flexible solar panel in the world. It is also very light because it does not contain glass or aluminum, as opposed to traditional panels, and it can be attached to any surface using screws (piercing just the Teflon that sticks out beyond the panel). The result was a flexible photovoltaic surface that can be installed on curved surfaces. It doesn't shine like glass: the texture is similar to zinc, with a dark color similar to graphite.

The IAAC developed the project, installed it in Madrid, achieved widespread attention in the media and won the People's Choice Award. After that experience in Madrid, I had the opportunity to show our project in Shanghai, during the International Exposition, as a guest of the Barcelona Design Center. After that presentation, different Chinese groups showed interest in our houses.

Leilei Chan and Pilar Clavo, who had spread the word about the

activities at the Barcelona pavilion in Shanghai, introduced us to
a group of Chinese investors. We began putting together master
plan for an island near the city, where the idea was to build a self-
sufficient environment that would include food production and
solar houses. In a recent visit to China, we began to evaluate the
use of bamboo in housing, because it is a rapid-growth material and
it can be cut into thin sheets to create panels and sections similar
to the ones we needed to build the homes we designed.
Through this project, we want to bring innovation in the design
of self-sufficient buildings to society in the quickest way possible.
In the digital world, innovation is transferred to society nearly
automatically through information networks.
Why is innovation in architecture and in housing so slow?
Google updates their algorithm at least once every few months.
Apple updates their computer and iPhone models at least once a
year. The automobile industry produces new versions of its models
every five years. The construction industry changes how buildings
are built every twenty-five years, and that's an optimistic estimation.
We need to carry over the innovation from the information society
into the construction industry.
Francis Ford Coppola says that he managed to buy his freedom to
produce his own films, removed from the big movie studios that
are directed by managers who evaluate a film's worth in terms of
the increase their company's worth on the stock market. Money is
cowardly. In cinema and in real estate development. It would be
fitting to find the formula to connect directly with people, in order
to be apprised of their desires and hopes for their homes and their
living environment.
But now, given the brutal crisis of values concerning what we
should do with the resources we have and how we should organize

our habitat to live better, consuming less energy, there is no doubt that investments will need to be made in innovation with respect to the human habitat. It is the first step toward being more efficient in interacting with the world. Culture generates more culture. Innovation creates more innovation. Creating self-sufficient buildings, even if there is no demand in the market, because they are unfamiliar, is a way of opening up new economic territory.

PRINTING BUILDINGS

Creating objects using a digital printer is already a reality; and people are currently working on digitally printing buildings. Berok Khoshnevis[17], at the University of Southern California, has been working for years on the creation of building-scale plotters installed in cranes with the capability of literally building houses or blocks apartments. He studies pen points that release precise quantities of ink, in a controlled manner, in order to allow for writing on paper. In the same way, the right printer head, with the ability to pour a material similar to concrete, with a precisely calculated thickness, would be able to print building-scale structures. A parallel printer head might even introduce the necessary cables or conduits for the building systems.

IF ARCHITECTURE IS A LANDSCAPE,
THEN BUILDINGS ARE MOUNTAINS

But buildings are not architecture if they can establish a precise relationship with their location and the environment in which they are built. High-rise buildings are functional accumulators, such that cities can multiply their extension by a factor of n through the accumulation of one floor on top of another. However, buildings don't necessarily have to be parallelepipeds. Modern architecture exalted abstract, Euclidian geometry, moving beyond the classic styles of the past. The development of fractal geometry by Benoît Mandelbrot[18] allowed for a numerical description of the structure of a tree, a cloud or a broken coastline. It also allowed for the design of complex surfaces in buildings, which have been produced using parametric design tools that admit the creation of a number of different elements with the same basic form, introducing slight "parametric" variations to make them distinct.

In recent years, aided by new geometries, architecture has sought out a new relationship with nature and the landscape around cities, building what have come to be known as "Landscrapers"[19].

As opposed to positioning itself on the landscape, architecture wants to become a landscape.

"If architecture is a landscape, then buildings are mountains,"[20] we argued at the end of the nineties. In Dènia, a town located on the Mediterranean coast, there were plans to rebuild the volume of a mountain in an old quarry, in order to build a spa resort and create commercial activity, along with urban services in its interior. Based on that idea, I developed a project that proposed building a building-mountain where the access points were located along the exterior surface of the reconstructed volume, thereby also creating an urban park and a center for urban activity. I also designed a building-mountain in Wroclaw (Poland) that included a convention center and a hotel as part of the city's candidacy for the Expo2012. A number of cities have expanded until they have come up against quarries or geological structures that have been used in the past to obtain materials for the construction of the city. This interaction between the city and its environment should allow for new forms of construction, closer to the natural structures that fractal geometry has helped us discover.

FORM FOLLOWS ENERGY

Living things are the product of natural evolution over thousands of years. They are specialized organisms that are adapted to their environment; their basic principle is fulfilling their basic functions (be born, grow, reproduce and die) with a minimum consumption of energy. Their shape responds to their adaptation to the environment to make them more efficient as a part of an ecosystem where there is mutual feedback from all of the parts.

Buildings have only been around for five thousand years.

For centuries, Man has built using the materials found near the most appropriate areas of the territory, with the aim of deriving a maximum of resources from his surroundings.

Up until the end of the 20th century, architecture fulfilled the function of representing the values of its promoters based on certain constructive codes based on the language of classical architecture, using capitals, friezes or arches, integrated through axes of symmetry, scale relationships, etc.

In classical architecture, form follows representation.

In the 20thcentury, the development of new materials like concrete, steel and glass, allowed for changing the rules of construction. In contrast to the historical model based on load-bearing walls, where the form of a building was directly related to its structure, the free design of the ground plan allows for increased flexibility in terms of a building's use. And its representation as well.

The "machine age" allowed for imagining buildings that "breathed" artificially and were fed by electrical systems. A new physical structure and a mechanical system —the elevator, which definitively cemented the possibility of vertical growth in buildings— led to new architectural paradigms. "Form follows function," asserted the *Bauhaus*[21] school. Glass and steel promoted a generic,

international architecture, that had to resolve its relationship with its surroundings. Using mechanical systems, they produced more or less energy, and controlled their surroundings without a thought for the associated energetic costs. This model has obviously run its course. At present, we are faced with the challenge of putting up buildings that return to emerging naturally from the place where they are built. Buildings that use a maximum of resources in order to ensure their energetic self-sufficiency, to obtain water from the surroundings and to recycle their waste material. This has to be done based on two principles. On the one hand, a detailed analysis of the systems and resources available in a specific place. And on the other, using design as a mechanism to resolve the combination of all of the functions the building needs to provide and the mechanisms that need to be developed, with the aim of consuming as few resources as possible for the building's operation.
Likewise, technology allows for integrating new resource production systems (energy, food, goods) to make buildings productive.
Buildings should be produced artificially and managed naturally. That is why they need to develop their own metabolisms, as a result of the combination of those two variables.
If in the 20th century architecture was altered due to a change in its structure, in the 21st century, architecture will be altered because of a change in its metabolism
In order for buildings to become self-sufficient, they must first be intelligent. They need to develop intelligence systems, built in to their structure. The idea is not to design traditional buildings and equip them with control systems, or solar panels on the roof. It is a question of defining new paradigms that combine function, energy and information in a single habitable structure.
Buildings as organisms. Cities like natural systems.

PHOTOSYNTHESIS AND ENERGY

In collaboration with Gerard Passola, known as *Doctor Tree*, we analyzed how to learn from the metabolisms of trees and other living things to structure the metabolism of buildings.

Trees are organisms that capture energy through their leaves by means of photosynthesis. The energy efficiency of a leaf is about 25%. In the case of real sunlight, where only 45% of the light is photosynthetically active, the maximum theoretical efficiency for the conversion of solar energy is about 11%. At present, however, plants do not absorb all of the sunlight that come in (due to reflection, the requirements for the respiration of photosynthates, and the need for optimum levels of solar radiation). In 2010, the most efficient solar cell had an efficiency of 23%. It is only a question of time, and of development in nanotechnology, until we reach the efficiency of natural systems, or even surpass them.

The leaves on a tree transform light energy into chemical energy in the form of raw sap in the roots. They use chemical energy to synthesize organic fuel molecules, which can be "stored" as carbohydrates. The physical structure of the branches and the trunk and the logical structure by way of which the information is sent through the woody conduits is the same. In architecture, there are examples that are oriented in the same way. The columns under the square in Barcelona's Park Güell have a physical structure and serve as a water collection system. The structure of the Media House combined the physical structure with the electric structure and the data structure in the same section.

Modern architecture separated systems into differentiated layers, whereas nature generally tends to integrate systems, for increased efficiency. In the case of trees, the structural connection with the ground is carried out in the roots, which have a similar branching structure to the crown. On the surface of the root hairs, outgrowths at the tip of a plant's roots, minerals are absorbed and water is taken in. The tree works like a pump, capable of sending the elaborated sap toward the crown and transforming its energy into fruit. All of that without being connected to a far-off electricity network. Maximum local efficiency.

In years to come, buildings will work in a similar way. On the one hand, they will maximize their relationship with their surrounding in order to use passive resources in an active way.

The best energy is the kind that is not consumed. And on the other hand, technology will be used in a subtle way to manage the resources needed for a building to function, in an organic and efficient manner.

Therefore, whereas in the past a building's form followed its representation, and in the 20th century form followed function, in the 21st century, form has to follow energy, using natural patterns for the design of buildings and cities, just like nature has always done.

3. City Block
(1,000)

What kind of potential could be derived from the interaction of a number of buildings in an urban system that promotes the distributed management of resources? How can energy be generated and stored in cities?

City blocks are units of urban structure, marked off by roads, which accumulate urban functions in the form of buildings. Ildefons Cerdà, the father of Barcelona's Eixample[1], called them "Intervies". The geometric definition of city blocks emerges from the optimum balance between the surface area that a city dedicates to public space and the surface area destined for human activities. The grid defined by that structure, and which houses mobility in a city, is conditioned by territorial and environmental questions, in seeking out the optimum urban integration in a specific territory.

New York was defined by a structure of rectangular *city blocks*[22] with dimensions of about 200 by 60 meters, perpendicular to the Hudson River. Barcelona was defined by square city blocks of 113 by 113 meters, with chamfered street corners and situated parallel to the sea and the Collserola mountains; the enlargement of Taipei was developed in the nineteen fifties based on large 500 by 500 meter blocks with interior passages. City blocks and their density are the units that define the rhythm of a city.

In historic cities, buildings are connected by party walls creating compact physical units that attempt to maximize the built volume in a dense urban fabric. In urban areas with detached housing, a city block may contain a number of separate housing blocks with green space in between, the product of the urban culture that emerged in the nineteen twenties. In the suburbs of large cities, a block is made up of a number of detached or semi-detached houses, dissolving the relationship between occupation and emptiness from historic cities into a habitable texture built at the rhythm of the automobile. City blocks with single-crop house farming. Green areas can be concentrated in large urban parks or they can be dissolved into the built structures of the blocks. In the case of Barcelona, Cerdà, in his hygienist vision oriented toward homogenizing good living conditions for all inhabitants, proposed that every city block should have a green space in its interior. Every building had access to mobility infrastructures on its urban front and to green spaces from the rear façade. Green spaces at a scale of 1 to 1,000. For its part, New York has hardly any green spaces in the interior of its city blocks, but it has Central Park. Barcelona's green spaces, on the scale of a city block, or on a city-wide scale, like in New York, are different models for organizing elements of human habitability. The functional content of a city block depends on which functions are addressed at each scale within the city. The mixture of functions in a city block promotes urban complexity and reduces mandatory mobility for part of the population. From the point of view of management, city blocks are units that allow for a direct relationship between private entities, individuals or communities without crossing through public space. Unlike buildings, city blocks do not possess their own legal entity. However, they can allow for creating units with energetic and environmental resources that can be managed collectively, with a strong social base, in a more effective way than on the scale of a building.

Every city incorporates blocks with different dimensions, uses and densities, built up over the course of its history, which, when grouped together, create the structures of neighborhoods.

DENSIFICATION OF CITIES

In 2009 I was invited to Phoenix by the previous president of
the Frank Lloyd Wright Foundation, Phil Allsopp, who promotes
research and projects oriented toward the promotion of increased
density and urbanity in American cities. Phoenix and Scottsdale
are radical examples of suburban cities built in the United States
during the 20th century. Every individual lives in a house with
a little plot of land around it, without any relationship to the
neighboring plots. Each dwelling is an island, within a territorial
magma structured by roads. Every dwelling has a small-scale green
space, which each owner cares for painstakingly, and the point of
social interaction is the golf club. A large private green area.
The question being discussed was how to achieve more urban
density and greater social interaction. At some point in the near
future, the United States will have to deal with the reform of
its suburban territories, for the first time in history. They were
urbanized in a most energetically inefficient way, at a time when
the price of energy was very low.

In an opposite direction, Barcelona has begun the process to free
up a maximum of surface area in the interior of its city blocks,
occupied by old industry or by buildings that carry out commercial
activities, built during a phase of when Cerdà's blocks were further
densified. Freeing up those spaces goes hand in hand with the
creation of parks, or the construction of social infrastructures under
the street level. In fact, it is a great strategy.

Many cities still only take into consideration the suitability of
putting up buildings above street level. What is built below ground
level is nearly always only evaluated according to a different kind
of regulation, like fire codes or regulations on economic activities.
In the process of densifying cities, building spaces destined for

infrastructures or facilities under street level seems like an obvious strategy. The limitations will be determined by security conditions and habitability.

SELF-SUFFICIENT CITY BLOCKS IN BARCELONA
Resource supply systems have to be designed to account for peaks in demand.
If the city blocks in New York, Barcelona or Paris had to produce locally all of the energy that they consume, their functional diversity would mean they would need fewer production infrastructures because the consumption in different buildings occurs at different times during the day.
Monofunctional buildings are more inefficient because, if they need to produce energy locally, there will be high peaks of demand (which is what the system is calibrated for) and other moments when very few resources will be consumed.
A detached apartment building will have higher energy consumption rates at night or on weekends than during the day. However, during business hours, work centers and businesses consume more. If functional units with greater diversity are created, consumption rates can be balanced, because it will be more diversified over time.
Therefore, diverse city blocks will be more efficient than monofunctional ones.
A prototypical city block[23] in Barcelona has an area of approximately 10,000 m². The average building height is 24 meters, and the buildable area measures around 30,000 m².
In Barcelona proper (not counting the Zona Franca) there are 10,235 city blocks. A building, with mixed uses and a 70/30 proportion between housing and work centers, will show an

average energy consumption of 1,400,000 kWh and 760,000,000 kilocalories each year. If we imagine covering all the roofs in the block with a high-efficiency photovoltaic system, with an average efficiency of 23%, which is currently possibly, it can be assumed that 65% of the energy needed by the city block per year could be produced. If photovoltaic systems were also used on the façade, the electricity production could be incremented between twenty and thirty percent. It is still insufficient locally producing the entirety of the required electrical energy.

The production of energy in buildings, the sum of electricity and hot water, should be carried out based on a hybrid system that would probably include geothermic systems, photovoltaic systems, and as the case may be, mini wind farms and biomass systems.

RECYCLING BUILT CITIES

Urban energetic self-sufficiency will be achieved if resources are produced locally and if pre-existing resources are better conserved. In coming years, there are no large-scale migratory processes foreseen for Europe or the United States. Economic growth in emerging countries like India, Brazil, Russia, South Africa and the United Arab Emirates, the consolidation of China as a super power and the economic crisis in the Western world, will mean that urban development in Europe and the United States will be more based on recycling than on the extension of the urban fabric.

Any new growth will be an opportunity to define self-sufficient structures on the neighborhood scale or city-wide. The challenge lies in remodeling cities, in order to make them more efficient.

In Barcelona, and other European cities, there are enlargements built in the 19th century that we could qualify as monumental, which are unlikely to suffer large-scale transformations in their

solar roofs

urban orchard

housing
fab lab
equipments
public facilities

neighborhood heating

water recicling

electric car

The self-sufficient city block; it produces food, energy and things

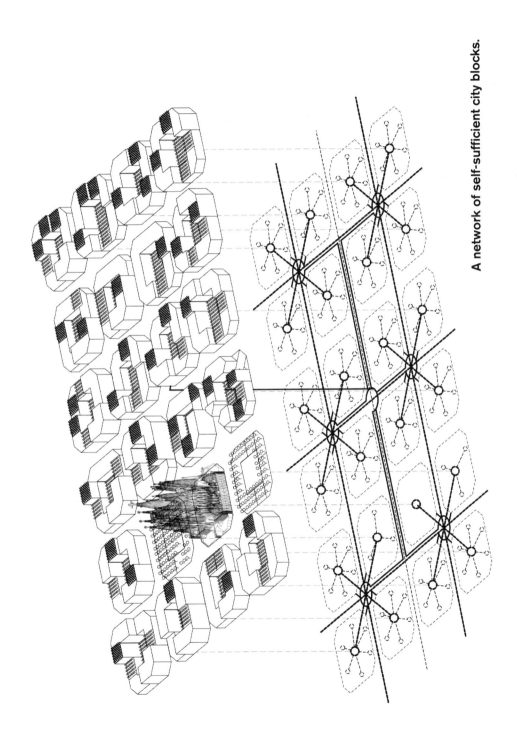

A network of self-sufficient city blocks.

exterior physical structures. They are a part of the city's image and its brand; as such, they will be refurbished as opposed to being recycled. However, there are other areas in cities that need to be renewed. And of those areas, the ones with the most economic value and the ones that will concentrate new economic activities related to the information society, are the ones that can potentially be transformed toward self-sufficiency, especially as a result of private initiatives.

Of the 498 city blocks in Barcelona's Eixample, 115 are located in the 22@ district, in Poblenou. This neighborhood, along with any number of neighborhoods and areas dedicated to technological activity, especially ones that include housing, commerce and workplaces, have the potential to be transformed into self-sufficient zones The 22@ Plan provided each city block with a special planning unit.

In its day, the planning allotted for a maximum density and a functional organization. But it did not prescribe an urban form based on alignments, as was the case in the 19th century or throughout the 20th century in historic cities and many urban developments.

A fixed height for buildings is becoming, increasingly, an irrelevant element in urban design.

In the case of 22@, both the existence of industrial structures to be preserved and the transformational dynamic that is characteristic of our culture, which moves beyond a closed, pre-established urban form, have meant that each city block in the neighborhood has taken on a different edificatory structure. That is good news. However, on rare occasions up to the present have there been brilliant solutions using unrestricted volumes for environmental purposes. The construction of city blocks using new principles based on self-sufficiency can promote changes in this direction. Self-sufficient city blocks will, in turn, create energy networks from one to another. And some of them, which include monumental complexes, will contribute another kind of energy to the system, through the economy derived from tourism.

LOCAL ENERGY PRODUCTION SYSTEMS

Energetic self-sufficiency can be achieved, as we have said earlier, through the generation of energy using a number of different systems to cover the annual energy needs for a building or a community. The scale of 1,000 people in a city block allows for implementing different technologies which are economically efficient and which derive the maximum benefit when they are set up in intelligent networks that manage the production and consumption for different properties, using systems like the Energrid.

Photovoltaic systems produce electricity using surfaces that transform solar energy into electricity. Traditionally, they have been installed on the roofs of buildings using panels comprising a number of cells. Transparent photovoltaic surfaces also exist which can be installed on top of window panes. The efficiency of photovoltaic systems, i.e., the capacity for producing energy of each panel surface, will increase in coming years with the use of technologies that include nanomaterials, which can be applied by way of different techniques, including painting, to nearly any surface. It is fundamental that building's energy production systems be managed using control systems that allow for proper maintenance. A self-sufficient building that is not maintained will stop working in no time, and it will become solar junk.

Another way of producing energy involves the use of thermosolar panels, which serve to produce hot fluid (water or oil) which can be used for heating purposes or for sanitary hot water. The production of electricity using hot water has been studied experimentally in small-scale structures.

Geothermal science allows for obtaining water at a constant temperature all year round, using tubes embedded in the ground. In winter, the fact that the water supply that is at 17 degrees means that when water needs to be heated, it is already be warmer than the ambient temperature. In summer, it means cooling it that much less for air conditioning systems. Finally, geothermal energy allows for other solutions in terms of building design, which is even more interesting. It can be used to cool or heat air, and as an air conditioning system, through a building's double skin.

Likewise, a number of cities make use of geothermal water from underground, which allows for extracting hot water at between fifty and eighty degrees Celsius. This water is added to centralized hot water networks and is sometimes used in thermal spa facilities. In extreme situations, like in Iceland, groundwater emerges as steam and allows for the direct generation of electricity.

The hot water produced by biomass boilers can be used very effectively in city-block-scale or neighborhood-scale plants. These plants may burn woodchips, straw or wood pellets. The key to their operation is supplying the resources to be burned. Logically, the energy consumed in transporting materials also has to be included in the calculation of the generation of CO_2. Biomass is considered a neutral system from the standpoint of CO_2 emissions into the atmosphere, because it is assumed that the emissions are equivalent to the amount that the vegetable elements eliminated as they were growing.

Current systems for the production of energy using biomass

are much more efficient for heating water than for producing
electricity, with efficiency rates of 60% versus a mere 30%.
However, it is a field with a broad potential for development based
on other systems, like pyrolysis, which decomposes woodchips
in the absence of oxygen and allows for heating water to very
high temperatures, which can produce electricity in a turbine, in
addition to producing biochar and other elements that result from
the decomposition of biomass atoms.

The combination of a different energy production systems and the
increased insulation in buildings to decrease energy expenditure
in the day-to-day operations, are two key strategies to achieve
an annual zero balance in the energy production for city blocks.
The most efficient systems are the ones where spikes in demand
produce smaller differences with respect to the regular supply.
Using micro-networks in buildings that require a stable supply
of energy, like hospitals or public pools, allows for maintaining a
constant operating base and reducing the variance between peaks
and valleys in supply.

STORING ENERGY IN CITIES

In order to create off-grid city blocks, which do not depend on the
energy network, we will have to guarantee massive energy storage
so that it can be supplied on cloudy days when there is no wind,
something which is not yet economically viable. In the same way
that the Internet has servers that store information, and from which
household terminals request data when they want to download
pictures or videos, energy systems in cities should also have
systems for storing energy.

Energy can be stored locally, whenever the building is producing
energy that it does not consume. When a wind power system

works during the night, in many cases it has to get rid of energy because it cannot be consumed. Photovoltaic systems also produce and excess of electricity during peak exposure times in summer months. And small-scale biomass plants can produce energy constantly is the are supplied with the appropriate raw materials. In recent years there has been work on storing energy in the form of hydrogen, which is later recovered through the use of fuel cells. However, the development of the electric car and the creation of a secondary market for used batteries (when can no longer store 80% of their capacity, as happens with cell phones) can allow for the creation of racks of car batteries in building basements to store energy when it is being produced and cannot be consumed. And electric vehicles will be used as energy storage systems, that can to transfer energy into dwellings when necessary.

Compressed air is another technology that is being tested and there are even prototypes for automobiles that are powered using this technology.

Cities with large height differences in their orography have a potential energy storage solution in mini waterfalls on a closed circuit, similar to traditional hydraulic systems.

City blocks have the right dimensions for creating "energy condominiums" within cities. In any case, an intelligent network will be necessary for managing this great potential diversity with respect to the generation and consumption of energy, and it will allow for a number of city blocks to act in conjunction.

NEW SPATIAL ORGANIZATIONS FOR WORK
Whereas cities build habitable structures the respond to the way of living, relating with others, and working that is characteristic of each particular time period, workplaces –their location and

accessibility– are key to organizing people's daily lives. Housing follows work.

Urbanization processes in Europe, America or China are linked to their industrialization processes. At the beginning of the 21st century, in countries like the United States, 1% of the population works in the primary sector, 16% in the secondary sector, and 83% in the tertiary sector. More than 40% of work in the tertiary sector is done "on the network", which means that the worker's location is no longer a relevant factor. In fact, we are witnessing a growing phenomenon in which things are being produced locally again, but "local" can be almost anywhere. However, there is urbanization without industrialization in Africa, which creates immense social imbalances in cities that fill up with people who have nowhere to work.

Globalization has produced an urbanizing movement that has concentrated human beings in cities, in places where the global economy is developing. At the same time, the knowledge society and the Internet promote empowerment, a re-arming of citizens, who will be capable of doing nearly everything with their own two hands. Developed societies promote so-called "slow" movements, where as developing societies what to follow a lifestyle which has, in many cases, proven to be unsustainable in many so-called developed countries.

In any case, one of the fundamental axes of any economy is create values that can be competitive in the world. Developed economies are now faced with the need to go back to producing resources locally, as opposed to only leading global processes associated with knowledge, while the physical manufacturing of products takes places in emergent locations.

Local production is a guarantee of survival in situations of uncertainty like the present. Producing energy, especially, is a factor of local independence. Producing food and goods is a factor of the quality of life that generates economic and social progress. Whereas in industrial society, the figure of the worker-consumer was promoted, with the information society the entrepreneur-producer emerges. Citizens with initiative whose workplace is the net. That is where the resources are managed that are used to operate in the physical reality of our cities.

Information workers, therefore, tend to be independent contractors with business initiative. They manage their own time; they create business and lead productive systems.

The physical structure of networked businesses is discontinuous. The relationship employee-company-workplace-building is an obsolete relationship. That is why we are witnessing the emergence of new relationships between work and physical space, which should be formalized in coming years.

In 1998, I developed the study, *"El teletreball i els telecentres com factor de reequilibri territorial"*[24] ["Telework and Telecenters as a Factor in Territorial Readjustment"] with the anthropologist Artur Serra and the economist Francesc Solà. The idea in that case was to try to keep inhabitants from leaving rural areas, through the creation of physical infrastructures that would allow them to interact with the rest of the world. That process led to the development of the Telecenter Plan for Catalonia, which initially allowed for the collectivization of information technologies in rural areas.

Working in a network means that the people who are working can work at any time, from nearly any place. The old teleworking model was associated with desktop computers located in fixed locations, like people's homes. Working consistently from home creates a large number of difficulties related with the collectivization of work. Now, access to networks has been universalized and this interaction can take place from just about anywhere. All the same, people tend to organize themselves into communities. That is why we need to imagine new kinds of productive spaces.

In cities, we could imagine office buildings where city-dwellers gather together based on the kinds of resources they need (computers, plotters, laser cutters, 3-D printers) as opposed to their affiliation with the same company. Or generic spaces where the only shared characteristic is working in a network. As such, working close to home, cutting out the time lost to mandatory mobility, can increase people's efficiency and their quality of life. Discontinuous companies. Distributed companies.

Current regulations in many cities do not permit the existence of residences and workplaces in the same building. They explicitly forbid installing office space above housing space. As a result, sometimes there is a need to resort to irregular situations in order to respond efficiently to the speed of the economy and the changing conditions of our production systems.

The large housing blocks on the periphery of cities, built in a hurry during times of large migration flows (in Spain, France and China), which initially only contained housing, and which have begun incorporating public facilities, will probably also begin incorporating next-generation workplaces. If that happens, part of the "working class" will have the potential to become new entrepreneurs. Between those two situations, education and leadership capabilities will need to be promoted in those neighborhoods.

The "creation factories" set up in Barcelona where there used to be historic industrial warehouses are another examples of spaces that operate transversally in terms of people coming together, not because they work for the same company, but because the work in a similar way.

In traditional city blocks, we can imagine new workplaces, up near the rooftops, as a new space for professional collectivization among freelancers who work on the net. Commerce at street level, housing just above, and work under the roof. A new functional hybridism in cities, organized vertically.

FAB LABS[25]

Whereas the industrial economy promoted the concentration of production in large factories in order to supply millions of consumers all over the world with products, the information society encourages the production of anything, anywhere in the world, by sharing knowledge and using personal manufacturing machines. It was in this context that MIT launched the Fab Labs, fabrication laboratories that are a part of the *transversal* process that is characteristic of working systems.

In 2001 Neil Gershenfeld created The Center for Bits and Atoms, as a spin-off of MIT's Media Lab, which was directed by Nicholas Negroponte from its foundation in 1985. It was one of the centers that contributed to the investigation and dissemination of information technologies. The initial vision was to merge the world of telecommunications, computing and content, and transform the world through new kinds of relationships. With the advent of the World Wide Web and interactive information systems, that initial vision was fulfilled. Neil's background is in physics, and through the "Things That Think" consortium, created in 1995, he began investigating the interaction between information technologies and the physical world.

Hacker culture, Marvin Minsky's neural networks and interaction. I met Neil at the opening of the Media Lab Europe, a sort of franchise set up in Ireland, through which the Media Lab attempted to promote research projects in Europe, though it was ultimately unsuccessful. Neil was also studying different kinds of interaction between MIT and India, which resulted in the discovery that dissolving technological knowledge into the world could be more interesting than "franchising" it, or even than recruiting the most talented young people in the world to study at MIT.

In fact, whereas historically the most advanced knowledge and the most advanced machines were gathered at major universities, today, knowledge is very often accessible on the net and, more and more, machines are within everyone's reach.

That was how the first Fab Lab was set up in Norway, promoted by Haakon Karlsen, a shepherd with a global vision and an interest in art and technology. With Neil's help, the first laboratory was set up in an old barn. The first project involved developing sensors to put on his sheep in order to find out their location remotely.

From there, a network began to grow, informally, in different countries all over the world, and there are now more than 100 laboratories in 25 countries. Recently, a bill was proposed in the United States Congress to create 500 Fab Labs across the country as a way to encourage training, research and production based on new principles.

A Fab Lab is a production workshop where nearly anything can be made using digital manufacturing machines and knowledge that is shared over the net. Fab Labs promote a new kind of economy, that is produced locally. The production is on time, and on site.

If we imagine any design created in a particular place in the world, as opposed to producing it in another place, we might think of it as a production model where the design or the idea can come from the net. Although the production would be local using digital manufacturing systems.

The machines used in a Fab Lab allow for building from a small computer to a house. Just about anything. A small computer can be made by milling the circuits on a copper plate and soldering on the different electronic components and the microprocessor. 3-D printers, manufactured by the Fab Lab, can also be used for printing; large wood panels can be cut with a large-scale milling machine to make furniture or, the parts of a house can be manufactured, or metal pieces can be cut with a laser cutter or a water jet to make structures or the parts of a bicycle.

Advanced design is a new production method that connects us with the medieval traditions of craftsmanship, because the designer manufactures the products him or herself. We can imagine dozens of new formats for micro-enterprises capable of supplying products to millions of people. During a recent lecture at Telefónica's corporate university, I was asked why I thought people would want to make their own chairs, when Ikea chairs are cheaper. The industrial model has been based on a limited number of producers and a great many workers who earn money in order to buy things. Buying a mass produced chair lets you own a chair in exchange for handing over money. The manufacturer receives your money and retains the knowledge of how to make the chair. But a person who manufactures a chair in a Fab Lab, gets the chair and retains the knowledge of how to make it. And, based on that knowledge, he or she may decide to make a table, or a wardrobe, or a house.

There is no knowledge included in the price of an industrial object, there is only the material and its function. In the so-called information society, people need to know how to make things. Because making one thing sets you on the path to making others. An industrial chair may have a low price, but the manufacturer retains the fundamental value.

In this process of adding value to the processes proposed by the self-sufficient city, possessing the knowledge of how to produce things will lead directly to the production of other things.
In Barcelona's Fab Lab, coordinated by Tomás Díez, we have carried out a number of experiments. In 2009, the Fab Kids program began, directed by Nuria Díaz. One of the experiments we proposed was asking a group of twelve-year-old kids what kind of objects they wanted to make. The piece they chose was a skateboard. They made a wooden mold. The kids glued a number of layers of wood together with glue and pressed them into the mold; then the wood was cut into the right shape with the milling machine and they used a laser to engrave the names and logos of their favorite bands into the wood.
"Can I buy your skateboard?" I asked one of the kids.
"No. I can't sell it," he said.
"Why not?" I asked.
"Because it's mine," he answered.
"What do you mean?" I insisted.
"It's mine. I made it," he replied.

We relate with things —a kilowatt, a tomato, a skateboard— when we make them ourselves, as opposed to buying them in a supermarket. They are products that are associated with knowledge. A new type of material relationship.
In fact, the interest in the origin of things and the traceability of the material history of objects is one of the direct consequences of the promotion of self-sufficiency. Everything we use has a material history. With an associated process, and with associated social, economic and environmental values. A new information economy should provide information and transparency with respect to

the values that are associated with any kind of product. From a kilowatt, to a tomato or a skateboard.

Just like animals have names, trees and objects should have them too. That way, we would be able to know about the social, energetic and economic process that lies at their origin. The aim is to guarantee the suitability of the processes associated with an object, beyond whether it is affordable or not.

The Fab Academy program was created in association with the Fab Lab; it is a distributed university, where the campuses are the different Fab Labs all over the world. It is a distributed university, not a distance university, because there is a physical, though discontinuous place where it takes place. Every Wednesday, one of the leading international experts in different areas related with manufacturing offers a videoconference, and during the week students work and do research with the help of a local instructor. They follow the hyperlocal model, based on a strong social and technological infrastructure established in a community that works because it is part of a global network.

Fab Labs are infrastructures on a neighborhood scale that allow for advanced education and distributed manufacturing in nearly any place in the world. At the Barcelona Fab Lab, we managed to garner the support of the Spanish Agency for International Development Cooperation, to launch a program that allowed us to choose two young people from Ethiopia and two from Peru, provide them with training for a year at the Fab Academy and then help them economically so that they could set up laboratories in Addis Ababa and Lima, respectively. The purpose is for them to train other people and to promote new economic forms based on inventions and locally produced initiatives. However, we also recognize an emergent economy in our own cities. In American and European cities, anywhere where we think we practice advanced economies, and where everything probably worked because we were advanced consumers as opposed to producers.

Barcelona underwent an industrial development in which the city blocks in the Eixample housed a large number of industrial establishments, especially in Poblenou. Some of the factories are still inexistence, and some have been recycled into commercial buildings, offices, learning centers, storage facilities, or others. The city blocks always had a hybrid characteristic, including places for work, for commerce and for rest. Embedded in the physical structures of Barcelona city blocks to serve as new formats for education, research and production, in outlying neighborhoods or in the historic fabric of former villages incorporated into the city, Fab Labs can create a transversal network to promote open innovation among inhabitants of all ages, and to stimulate the emergence of new economic activities linked to invention and on-demand manufacturing. That is why we should move from Fab Labs toward Fab Cities. Cities that manufacture based on the new principles of sharing knowledge globally and producing resources locally. Cities that promote the knowledge economy.

LOCAL FOOD PRODUCTION

The production of food at the scale of a city block is an emergent initiative in cities. In recent years a number of small-scale projects have been developed, rooted more with marketing than in a strategy aimed at what is possible.

Green roofs are a very valid technical solution in that they provide good isolation, they can retain rainwater to avoid saturating rainwater networks during storms and the stimulate a more natural landscape on the roof terraces of urban buildings.

In Barcelona, beyond the roofs of historic or monumental buildings, roofs are an infrautilized territory that could be functionally and environmentally activated perfectly well. In the Eixample, on the one hand, more than 50% of roofs are flat and they do not have a definite use. In the case of housing blocks built in the nineteen seventies in neighborhoods like Ciutat Meridiana, on the other hand, the roofs are radically flat, as corresponds to the typology of an open-building housing block, and they can easily be transformed into microgardens.

Beyond the transformation of existing buildings, in a number of different cities in the world, the idea of a building-farm is being studied where vertical agriculture would be possible using hydroponic methods. This idea makes sense in the case of global overpopulation, which could happen in 2050 when there may be as many as 10 billion people on Earth, 80% of whom will live in cities. When traditional farming environments reach their production limits, new ways of producing food may emerge that are similar to the vertical farms in cities. Doctor Dickson Despommier, a Columbia University professor, discussed this incipient idea in his book, *The Vertical Farm*[26].

Urbanization brought sanitation infrastructures to buildings and cities, and with them, the nutrients produced by buildings began to be carried off to treatment plants.

At present, the food cycle favors production that is carried out anywhere in the world using techniques and processes which remain unknown, in most cases. Those products are sent to cities, where they are distributed to the restaurants and homes where they are consumed. The residue from foodstuffs, whether or not it has been digested by people, is collected and taken to recycling plants, in the case of trash, or to treatment plants, in the case of sewage,

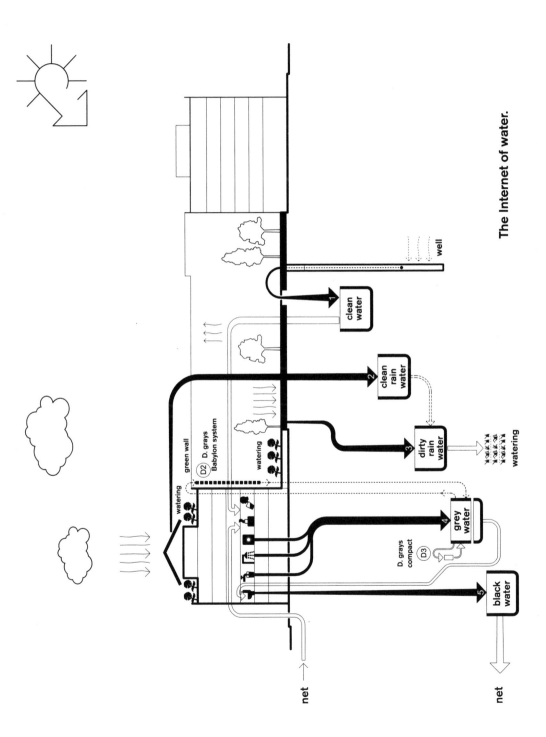

The Internet of water.

where, ideally, solid and liquid wastes are separated and both are returned to the life and food cycle as water for irrigation and fertilizers.

With the proposal for the local generation and consumption of energy, work can also be done toward local food production, based on a more intelligent management of the water cycle on the city-block level. Water can be classified into different qualities and stored according to its origin, whether it is purified water, rainwater from roofs, rainwater from the ground, grey water or black water. And, in turn, it can be reused, in the case of grey water, for watering or flushing toilets, and nutrients can be extracted to create fertilizer for the plants in surrounding areas.

We need to promote an Internet of water, *Hydrogrid* with a multiscalar scope, with structures that operate in the range of city blocks, neighborhoods, and cities as a whole.

The quality that water has to have in order to be qualified as "potable" has varied over time. It will probably evolve to the point that in the case of big cities that are far away from large fresh water reserves may need to install small water-treatment plants near consumption areas.

In recent years, we worked with the engineer Jochen Sheerer on the development of a project to create intelligent networks for local water consumption and the reutilization of grey water and black water, in the most efficient way, recovering a number of chemical elements such as phosphorous, which exists dissolved in water in places where there is human habitation, but is scarce in nature. Man as a biochemical transformation machine. Buildings as generators and managers of environmental resources.

In coming years, we need to emphasize the need to preserve the agricultural land across which cities have been growing to create their metropolitan areas. To turn producing food, selling food and eating food into a process of celebrating local culture.

And, if necessary, to research other ways of producing food based on knowledge and its relationship with disciplines like healthcare and building design.

4. Neighborhood
(10.000-100.000)

Within the city, neighborhoods are the organs in the built body.
They are the urban structures that define the territory that a person
can cover in a natural repetitive way, by his or her own devices.
Their dimensions are connected with human physiology. They are
communities that connect us with the ancestral character of tribes,
with which human beings have lived for hundreds of years. Well-
built cities encompass very different neighborhoods. Places with
definite social and cultural identities that celebrate their differences
with differentiated urban structures, social events and economic
activities, which maintaining continuity with the common territory
of the city.
Neighborhoods are units within the city with uniform physical
characteristics. They are part of the urban magma that emerge
either as a result of the development of historic settlements, or due
to the development of rapid growth in a particular moment
in history.
Neighborhoods are territorial units where the physical proximity
among inhabitants can allow for relationships based on the
physical exchange of resources. Whereas a city block is an urban
unit, where physical contiguity implies that neighbors are the first
potential candidates for any interaction based on mutual benefit,
neighborhoods are entities that include larger units than dwellings
and their immediate surroundings, where the public and communal
quality of the urban phenomenon comes to light. Neighborhoods
have churches, libraries, markets, sports centers and green areas;
as such, they define the first scale of community association that
exists in cities.

According to the hyperhabitat structure, which explains the organization of the human habitat based on a multiscalar system, the 10,000 scale is the last one where people can still perceive the territory as an extension of their dwelling.

In order for a city to be self-sufficient, its neighborhoods have to be. An accumulation of between 10,000 and 50,000 people can allow for any social community to approach energetic self-sufficiency, and create, for the large part, an ecosystem of functional relationships, allowing for living, working and resting. Neighborhoods, as units that contain 10,000 inhabitants or more, could themselves be seen as microcities in the interior of big cities. A neighborhood is a territory that can be crossed on foot in a maximum of thirty minutes. In fact, the "slow city" movement fixes the maximum number of inhabitant of a city that can adhere to the movement at 50,000.

The best cities in the world have clearly identifiable neighborhoods that act as poles for internal competition to lead in the dynamism of the city. The center of New York, Manhattan, is a paradigmatic case in that respect. Over the past thirty years, different areas, like Chelsea, have competed with the West Village to attract art galleries. Now, with the creation of the New Museum, the Lower East Side has created a new pole for competition. Chinatown, Harlem or Midtown are parts of an overall unity that has a differentiated cultural and functional identity.

Barcelona has 73 neighborhoods. A number of them have emerged from independent villages or small urban centers, which were transformed into one more unit in the built magma as the city became a metropolis. As such, many of them still possess a distinct, differentiated identity in their genetic material, which allows them to work like microcities where people live, work and rest, in the interior of the big city.

In other cases, during times of rapid growth in the city, neighborhoods are created on the periphery (like *Bon Pastor*) to respond to specific needs having to do with the workings of the city. In some cases (like *Ciutat Meridiana*) neighborhoods are built mote than 3,000 housing units where there is minimum commerce and not a single workplace. In other cases, like Bon Pastor, there are industrial neighborhoods where very few people live. In the center of the city (like in the *Eixample*), on the other hand, a large neighborhood was built that has been transformed, over time, into a mixed-use place where there are dwellings, commerce, workplaces, schools, leisure and everything that can be found in a city.

In the way, there are functionally hybrid neighborhood in the urban ecosystem as well as monofunctional ones that exist more as part of a bigger reality, to which they contribute a specific functionality, than as "cities" in and of themselves.

In cities that have experienced rapid growth based on migrations from rural areas to the city, like in a number of Chinese cities, the built volume of brand new neighborhoods can be as much as 80% in comparison to neighborhoods that have been in existence for 50 years or more. In that case, the relationships of identity and function are much more complicated. Those territories have been built based on decisions made from the top down, requiring decades to transform multiple sets of housing blocks into actual neighborhoods. Understood as multifunctional units with their own identities, they can contribute value and diversity to the city, beyond the fact of their mere existence.

LOCAL IDENTITY

In the first decade of the 21st century, the Internet has promoted globalization based on connections between people who have been able to exchange or trade in goods, or information, without regard for their physical location. In fact, India is home to a large quantity of technological services tied in with companies, especially American companies, that can carry out a number of different activities through information networks, when physical proximity is not an issue. The call centers for French or Spanish telephone companies can be located anywhere that a mass of people who speak the language can be found, but with much lower labor costs. The possibilities of learning about the world and creating exchanges associated with knowledge are never-ending. That is one of the great contributions of information networks.

Digitalization has made it possible for a number of content-related processes, like watching films or buying music and books, to be carried out remotely, both in space and in time. Social networks have allowed for meeting people all over the world and making "virtual friends". However, as we have said before, Internet has not changed our neighborhoods, or our relationships with our neighbors. In fact, the Internet can lead to the creation of insubstantial social interactions, as a result of chance meetings through photographs or videos on a website, as opposed to the positive social interaction that can improve people's quality of life. The physical proximity between people allows for developing the "neighborhood web" as a platform for promoting the exchange of resources among city inhabitants.

The industrial world, motivated by corporations oriented toward the production and sale of good, has promoted the identification of the basic needs to be satisfied with products that can be purchased individually. As such, mobility has been associated with the automobile that a person or a family needs to possess in order to be efficient, as opposed to evaluation the potential for relating public and private mobility and undertaking the appropriate investments at the right time. In my case, for over ten years I lived in the center of Barcelona and walked to work or used systems like the metro or taxis for longer-distance urban journeys. When I needed a car to leave the city, or to take a trip, I rented one. If we analyze the investments, the maintenance, the insurance and the parking costs, it only makes sense to buy a car in the case of high-frequency use or use in a family or in a group that makes collective travel easier. In the same way, the idea of "living" is associated with the need to buy a house, much more than with the idea of a "habitat" as a series of potentialities that an individual takes from the city, at the scale of a dwelling, a building, public space, a neighborhood, or the city itself, and which allow people to put together a specific, complete lifestyle. People live in a territory that we can recognize as our own. In fact, the design of a neighborhood allows for proposing a number of different scales for satisfying individual needs, which encompass all of the functions that can be carried out in a city, creating a more efficient and social structure.

SOCIÓPOLIS[10]

In 2002 I presented a proposal for the design and construction of a new neighborhood in the city of Valencia. The project was developed within the framework of the Valencia Biennial, directed by Consuelo Ciscar. It was a magnificent opportunity to investigate how new generation neighborhoods should be structured. Thirteen architects were selected for the project, and were asked to design a multi-functional building in the new neighborhood.

The architects we invited were Ábalos&Herreros, FOA, François Roche, Manuel Gausa, Greg Lynn, Willy Müller, MVRDV, Duncan Lewis, Lourdes García Sogo, Jose María Torres Nadal, Eduardo Arroyo and Toyo Ito. We redacted the master plan on the plot proposed by the city council. For lack of urban territory, it was laid out on farmland. It was high quality agricultural land, structured by a network of irrigation canals developed by the Muslims when they were living in Valencian territory before the reconquest.

Whereas urbanization means transforming agricultural or natural land into urban land, by tracing a network for collective mobility on top of it, installing infrastructures and creating urban plots with less surface area than the original division, to serve as the site for vertical construction, I proposed that the process be kept to a minimum: that it should be functional as opposed to structural.

I proposed that automobiles should be parked at the far end of the sector, near the existing traffic routes, and that the entire area should be for pedestrian use only. As such, the agricultural plots would literally serve as the plots for construction, whereas other agricultural plots would not house any buildings, and would maintain their activities. The result would look like a medieval system, with a series of built spaces and open spaces arranged with a large degree of continuity and density. From a functional standpoint, we created a table with the principle uses in cities and divided them into four categories: housing, work (which also includes commerce and leisure), facilities and infrastructures.

I proposed that each architect should design a building that would include housing (or other living arrangements, like rest homes) and two other uses. One building contained housing, a market and a recycling plant; another: housing, a day care center and an agricultural center; another: housing, a thermal power plant and a leisure center, etc. In this way, each building satisfied needs on a collective scale (100 or 1000) as opposed to an individual scale (1). We created a website where the architects sent in their initial sketches, and this led the projects to relate with one another, even allowing for a change in the location of one of the projects.

My position at the time became that of the "web master planner". This initial project resulted in an exhibition and a book editing in conjunction with the Architekturzentrum in Vienna, directed by Dietmar Steiner, and which served as the foundation for the development of the actual neighborhood, which began later on.

CITY PLANNING FOR URBAN INTERACTION

This project had a foundational character, because it led us to reflect on the multiscalar nature of the urban habitat. People don't live in their houses. The in habitat a continuum of spaces made up of their apartment, building, neighborhood or city, which allows them to satisfy their basic needs either individually or collectively. The location of facilities and other functional centers promotes or limits social interaction. A city is created by the number of interactions that occur among its inhabitants, especially in public space. The physical arrangement of dwellings, workplaces, leisure centers and facilities will foment or eliminate the potential for spontaneous physical encounters between neighbors, so that the creation of a feeling of community is either promoted or limited. If a neighborhood is considered to be a network of functional nodes that encompassed housing, work, services and infrastructures, then urban design allows for the physical organization of social interaction. A city where everyone lived in a capsule and no one interacted with their neighbors would not be a city. It would be more like a prison made up of individual suburbs, where everyone would be afraid of everyone else. On the level of governance, or on a cultural and economic level, the collective interest emerges from the interaction between people who engage in different activities and who have divergent interests, but who agree to live together as part of a community.

In 2003, it was decided that the initiative should become a reality, in the La Torre district of the city of Valencia. Following the principles laid out in the previous investigation, it was decided that the objective would be to accommodate a maximum number of people (to consume a minimum amount of territory) while maintaining a maximum of non-urbanized space within the city.

The land allocated for the proposal is limited by a network of high-capacity traffic routes, creating an agricultural island on the edge of the city. According to the usual practice, the sector would have been urbanized by the extension of the adjacent streets, creating a series of city blocks ready for building and broad green spaces. We decided, however, that at the beginning of the 21st century, it was a good time to think about how the city could be built based on new principles that would promote low-speed locally and where the resources from the surroundings would be incorporated into the project.

VALUE VS. PRICE

One Saturday afternoon, walking around the site, I met a man who was plowing the land with the help of a draft horse.

"What are you doing?" I asked him.

"I'm plowing the land," he said.

"Why?" I insisted.

"Well, I'm rich," he answered.

"Rich?" I questioned.

"Yes. Plowing a patch of land in the city of Valencia on a Saturday afternoon is something that money can't buy. It's priceless. That's why I'm rich," he explained.

This situation provides a clear explanation of the difference between value and price. Things have the price that is paid for them, which is fixed by the economic environment of a place. But value extends beyond economic circumstances.
Months earlier, I had attended an event at the monastery of Santa Maria de la Valldigna, with the participation of people from the cultural industry from all over the world, in the middle of the Valencian countryside. When the event was over, they took us on a walk toward a small hermitage, located about a kilometer away. More than two hundred, well-dressed people went walking through the fields of orange trees in flower, where the orange blossoms and the humidity of the terrain gave off an incredible sensation of spatial depth, despite the fact that it was just a "simple" grove of orange trees.

URBANIZE THE COUNTRYSIDE, RURALIZE THE CITY

For the design of the Sociopolis neighborhood, we organized a workshop in which we asked a number of citizens and students what they would like to see happen in front of their houses in their new neighborhood.
Cities are often too similar to one another, because urban planning is applied like a technical process, independently of social or cultural values or the importance of the landscape. Oftentimes, urban design, the construction of a city, arises solely in response to the desire to capitalize on an economic value, which places a structural limitation on the physical progress of the habitats in

which people live. Money, when there is any, is faint-hearted. As such, designing a neighborhood, building a part of a city, tends to be carried out with an eye on the problems that need to be managed in the present, as opposed to the social, cultural, and economic potential for the future.

In the workshop, the proposal stipulated that there should be a soccer field at the center of the neighborhood, as a space to promote social interaction among inhabitants of all ages. Sports as a transversal activity that promotes socializing within the community. The field was meant to serve as the starting point for a sports-related circuit, which would connect with other facilities, like swimming pools or an all-purpose track, to make it possible for people to exercise in the street. The existing rural roads were to be preserved, for the most part, because they constitute a structure that has been kept alive in the territory despite the passage of time. We could set up large urban gardens, preserving the existing agriculture. Not as a semi-industrial activity, but as a kind of social agriculture that will allow citizens to grow fruits and vegetables just outside their homes. The area was traversed by a network of irrigation canals that were set up by the Muslims who came over from Egyptian lands, more than a thousand years ago. The systems they built are characteristic of a people with advanced technical knowledge from a territory with impressive know-how in the use of water. The network of irrigation canals, which is still operational today, is based on splitting up the water flow that comes from the Turia River into a number of irrigation canals, which are grouped into seven watering communities that divide the water in proportion to the surface area that need to be irrigated. When there is a lot of water, everyone has water to spare; in periods of drought, everyone suffers equally. Water democracy. As such, in

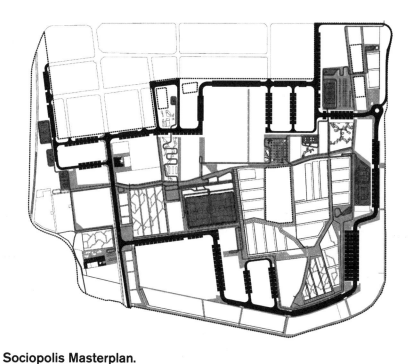

Sociopolis Masterplan.
Urban Emergence: A network of intersections
on the paths between homes and facilities.

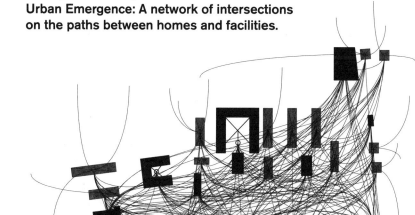

order to build on this farmland, we analyzed the irrigation canals, their distribution systems, and we drew up the surrounding neighborhoods and the optimum connectivity possible toward the outlying neighborhood of La Torre.

The network of irrigation canals is not only the foundation for agricultural activities. It also serves the basis for the oldest people's court in Europe, Valencia's Water Court, recently declared as a Intangible Cultural Heritage. In the past fifty years, more than half of the surface area supervised by the courts has disappeared as a result to the extension of the city of Valencia, which is literally burying the farmland. In the case of this project, protecting part of the agricultural land and restoring and rebuilding irrigation canals means protecting an intangible asset, the Water Court, which has met every Thursday in front of the Valencia cathedral for more than a thousand years.

However, not everyone has the same idea. At one time, there was a proposal to disconnect the new canals that we were planning to refurbish and rebuild from the traditional water supply coming from the Turia river, in order to create a kind of theme park, where it would look like the traditional system was being used, whereas it would actually be connected to the municipal watering system. Logically, we insisted on using the traditional techniques and watering systems to reconstruct the farming landscape inside the city.

In designing this neighborhood, the fundamental criterion was the preservation of a maximum surface area of non-urbanized land, the creation of a neighborhood with the maximum number of social housing units with high-quality design, the definition of the highest possible number of facilities and public space to allow for social interaction. All of that on a limited budget, given the social nature of the project.

After the final layout of the streets had been built, a perimeter road was defined to allow for access to all of the buildings from behind. That way, all of the buildings located along the circuit are situated "on the garden front", facing the large central park that occupied 40% of the surface area in the sector, creating a panopticon system of buildings. More than 50% of the area was left unpaved, uncovered by any impermeable surface in order to allow water to filter into the ground. In fact, when a territory is urbanized what happens, literally, is that agricultural land is buried under layers of asphalt that form the network of roads and the hard-surfaced city squares. We came across an interesting paradox in our neighborhood: we proposed the installation of a number of photovoltaic surfaces in public space in order to generate part of the energy that is consumed there. However, the proposal was not accepted because the City Council, which is the body in charge of receiving and managing that kind of infrastructure, does not have a body dedicated to managing energy. They do manage clean water, grey water, waste materials, circulation or logistics, but they do not manage public information networks or energy. Again, the two key systems in our society, information and energy, are positioned in the orbit of large corporations.

Sociopolis, on the other hand, houses more than three times as much land dedicated to public facilities than is required by law. These plots of land, located along the circuit, are reserved for buildings intended for social use (medical center, sports center, day care center, high school, arts center, music center, agricultural center) and, in many cases, subsidized housing will be built on the upper floors. It was a way of repeating the model from the initial project where the public facilities, at a lower height, promote internal mobility within the neighborhood. As a result, there are an innumer-

able amount of crossings and focal points in public space, creating an intermediate scale, between the containers made up of homes and businesses, and the large-scale buildings and green spaces. An urban environment without traditional city forms.
Social density, functional diversity and spatial culture.
It is a neighborhood, to the extent that there is enough density and functional diversity, and a structure for public space that promotes social unity. And it creates a city.

SOCIAL MINING

A number of studies have analyzed the city as an economic phenomenon; they use the diversity of economic activities in a neighborhood or in the city as a whole to measure its urban strength and its resilience. But there is a unit that is smaller than businesses or organizations: people. The city is full of inactive human resources. Educational models or work organization models in different cultures can promote or hinder whether people transform their potential into value for the economy of the city. In cities in developing countries, the informal economy is very often an important part of the urban economy. Bogotá serves as a paradigmatic example, with the existence of large-scale informal markets, like San Victorino, where families sell the products they produce in home workshops, and where a logistics platform was created to export a large portion of those products to countries like China or India. But, in large cities in developed countries there are also a large number of people with skills and talents who don't always conform to the "demands of the market", or who haven't had the ability to receive a proper education. The problem isn't what they know; it's that they don't know how to activate that knowledge socially and economically.

A person with specific knowledge, with the ability to carry out a task in the city, who hasn't been activated, is like a little underground oil well that has yet to be discovered and tapped into. They are intangible resources, which can disappear over time if they aren't activated. Immigration processes add knowledge and new attitudes to cities which, if they are given the opportunity, can enrich cultural heritage and knowledge, strengthening a city's DNA. Many of the innovative companies involved in the digital revolution in Silicon Valley were developed by immigrants or the children of immigrants. Especially in periods of crisis, part of a city's efforts should be directed toward promoting social innovation projects in neighborhoods, especially the most disadvantaged ones, or where people are most disconnected from the social reality of the big city, with the aim of creating mechanisms and lines of connection between people and their potential, and the city's production systems.

Beyond its building blocks, a city possesses social capital that is built from personal relationships during decades, which needs to be consolidated wherever it exists. And when we think about building a new neighborhood or a new city, it should be based on promoting interactions among its inhabitants and pushing for the construction of social relationships. A city is a social invention. A city is an idea. The interaction of all of the inhabitant's ideas of the city is what keeps it going on a daily basis.

THE SOCIOPOLIS URBAN GARDENS

The largest urban gardens in Spain were built all around the *Saboner* farmhouse. There are 300 plots that will be managed by people who live in the neighborhood and in surrounding neighborhoods, for the purpose of growing food.

With proper management of what is planted, the gardens can produce enough vegetables to feed a family for a year. This new agricultural social club took a lesson from the Parque de Miraflores, where community gardens were built on top of a garbage dump, which, in turn, was located on top of the remains of a Roman villa with historical agricultural structures. They created a real collaborative culture among farmers of different ages, children and young people who spend part of their time growing vegetables, as opposed to traditional urban leisure, managing public space in the city and building up a community.

Another successful model was created by the Barcelona City Council, which has a number of urban gardens in each district, built up around former rural farmhouses. The gardens sometimes have ten times as many requests as available plots, so that every so often they have to rotate the concessions awarded for their use.

SHARING INFORMATION IN THE NEIGHBORHOOD INCREASES EFFICIENCY IN THE CITY

There are also plans for Sociopolis to have its own high-capacity intranet. In the same way that companies have an intranet, why shouldn't a neighborhood have one? Why should we always have to depend on information services companies who are allowed to use networks in the streets, financed by developers' investments, free of charge?

Local networks of all kinds promote social interaction between neighbors and allow them to live more efficiently at a lower cost. Aside from physical infrastructures, neighborhoods can create their own collaborative networks, using information technologies.

The neighborhood website will be a basic platform for communities across the world. The neighborhood website allows for relating activities with inhabitants' resources on a larger scale, without associated physical spaces. For example, a lot of people have books at home. Traditionally, neighborhood libraries have been built so that people have access to books that they don't own individually. A networked neighborhood library allows for sharing all of the books that people own individually, which they choose to make available to their neighbors in exchange for access to other volumes. Any resource in a dwelling, any space (kitchen, office, leisure, rest) can have an equivalent on a neighborhood scale if information is offered to the community and if there is a network of people who are willing to contribute and taking back from the community.

In fact, interactions can be organized around resources that only exist on a neighborhood scale. As such, the users themselves can get together to organize sports competitions of all kinds within the neighborhood.

The existence of associations is an important characteristic of many towns. We might also imagine senior citizens cooking for young people, university students teaching children, professionals of different kinds helping out their neighbors, where the only currency is good will. Or in some cases, using time banking as a system for regulating these relationships. A network of people who share information about their resources and their possibilities, based on physical proximity, has an incredible potential for transforming the way cities operate in a lot of different aspects and increasing their social capital.

Whereas in recent years, the kind of society that has been promoted is one where everything is bought and sold, there are other mechanisms to determine the relationship between how things are used and the people in cities. Sharing, lending, or giving away are all possible ways of being able to use things without buying or selling them.

POPULAR INITIATIVES FOR NEIGHBORHOOD MANAGEMENT

Social unity in neighborhoods, where people know one another because they community is relatively small and because different generations of families have been interacting for years, can be activated through computing systems that allow neighbors to get to know one another and derive mutual benefit from their relationships.

Generalized fear, created consciously through the diffusion of certain news items, generated even more fear. Neighborhoods, as the limit of a dwelling's range of action, are the space for rebuilding confidence and interest in the collective interest.

There are a number of American cities where people are beginning to talk about "communities". And, in many of those cities, the territory was built up around the idea of individuality. A dwelling is a container in the form of a "house", air conditioning, a good refrigerator and a beautiful yard just outside the door. A group of houses, one next to the other, does not make a community.

That is why there has been talk of densifying the suburbs and creating mechanisms to generate social interaction.

The town scale, the scale of a community, should be reconstructed within cities. The city police should greet us by our names when they pass us in the street!

The neighborhood website project should be an application that is born in dense cities, like European cities, where there is a sense of *civitas*. They should probably be promoted by the city's "administrators" and conceived of as a tool that is available to inhabitants, like urban space. As such, there is a need for a new kind of civil leadership in Western cities that recognizes a new relationship with society.

At present, politics remind us too much of feudalism, where

whoever holds the power, wields it as a mechanism to control society much more than to promote it. Voting every four years is not enough. Politicians born in the Internet generation, when they come to light, will understand the value of promoting society as opposed to controlling it.

The revolution in countries on the southern side of the Mediterranean is a clear example of how control is no longer sufficient in the management of a new society. Social networks allow people to organize themselves. The leading cities in the 21st century will be the ones where citizens can work as a team, where they understand the value of the collective, as the sum of strong, free, motivated individuals.

In parallel to the neighborhood website, we also proposed creating a fiber optic cable network in Valencia, owned by the community, that would allow for networked computation.

The SETI program for the detection of UFOs is an example of how connecting thousands of computers, during times when they are not being used by anyone, allows for carrying out tasks that would be impossible to undertake with just one individual computer.

Artur Serra, an anthropologist and one of the leaders of the Internet 2 project in Catalonia with Sebastià Sallent (UPC), told us about the potential of distributed computation on a neighborhood scale, equivalent to the supercomputers in the most important scientific research centers.

Distributed computation. Distributed cooking. Distributed libraries. Distributed sports. Distributed education. Sharing resources in order to do more with less.

New paradigms for regenerating the city and building spaces for peer-to-peer social interaction, which has traditionally been associated with public space.

5. Public Space

What is public space like in the information society?
How is collective identity created in public space?
What is the point of a street in a hyperconnected world?
Public space in cities defines the protocols for cohabitation used by
a community to build a society. It is the place where the code lines
for social interaction are written, where the culture of belonging
and of urban identity is created. It is also the territory that houses
the infrastructures that make a city work.
From Athens to Rome. From medieval cities to cities in the New
World. From Cerdà to Le Corbusier. From Chandigarh to Brasilia.
From Phoenix to Dubai. The proximity of the buildings, the section
of a street, the relationship between buildings and infrastructures,
the urban elements that populate it, define the values based on
which social space in cities is meant to be constructed.
The construction of a city happens in the balance between a
political conception (the government of the polis) and efficiency in
resource management.
The density of a European city, or the dispersion of a Western
American city, are not only the products of the implementation of
technologies for collective urban mobility (metro) or individual
mobility (cars). They represent two different positions in the
construction of collective and individual spaces.
The urbanization processes begun in the 19th century allowed for
an extensive and integral deployment of systems for urban mobility
and the provision of resources to support the functions that are
necessary in cities. Streets and their infrastructures constitute the
metabolic system of cities, built using overlapping layers, and the
thin skin of which materializes public space in the city.

The construction of a city begins with an urbanization process that is only possible if there are structures in place to govern it. Joan Clos[27], the director of UN-Habitat, asserts that there are cities in the world without streets or urban infrastructures because their political systems are not stable enough to establish them. Building a street is not just accumulating a series of functional infrastructures. It is the supreme act of urban culture.

Barcelona has created its own model for the urbanization of public space over the last few decades. But it hasn't been spontaneous. Before the 1980s, when Oriol Bohigas[28] created Barcelona's Urban Projects department, when a street needed to be built the different urban elements were incorporated into the city independently. The head of the department in charge of street furnishings would place an order for benches and trash cans; the landscaping department would take care of trees and plants; the people in charge of surfacing would buy the paving stones for the sidewalks, the lighting department would deal with streetlights. All of these elements were installed together in public space to create a "street". The initiative of transforming the city through urban projects led an individual, an architect, to draw a space where people could interact, based on new values that were meant to be transmitted, which were emerging from the new system of democratic government. The "project" defined the codes for using the city based on the right combination of materials, urban elements, natural elements and lighting, and the relationship between mechanical mobility and pedestrian mobility with the recognition of pedestrian commercial axes and large avenues. Once the "project" had been defined, the transformation of the city could begin. There are cities in the world where social and economic progress is materialized in public space, in collective infrastructures. And there are others where the

accumulation of capital is manifested in the private sphere.
Now, with the advent of information technologies, the project of
public space will be more complex. The reinformation of cities
promotes a re-engineering process that will allow them to be more
efficient. *Smart cities* emerged simultaneously from the desire
to improve the efficiency of infrastructures in cities and from an
interest on the part of the most capitalized companies in the world,
information technology companies, in opening up new areas of
economic activity.

Instead of mechanical technologies, the city as a system needs the
knowledge that comes from the life sciences for its regeneration.
Cities are urban ecosystems developed by human beings, who are
a part of natural ecosystems. Whereas civil engineering was key to
structuring the first urbanization processes in the 19th century, and
architecture was key to the construction of buildings, neighborhoods
and cities in the 20th, today urban ecology is the fundamental
science for organizing the city informationally for the 21st century.
The actions that take place in cities, which is where most of the
world's population lives, are transforming our climate.

The consumption of resources in cities, the generation of waste
material, the contamination of the air, are all the result of an old,
obsolete system which needs to be infused with new paradigms
based on the principles of networked self-sufficient cities.

As such, the organization of life in the territory, and the
construction of space, initially based on a settlement model and
later on public space design, are key structural decisions in the
development of activities in cities. The design of public space in
new cities and the refurbishment of existing public space should
come from new knowledge that combines environmental aspects
with technological and cultural ones.

The technologies that contribute intelligence to this urban re-engineering should be based on new operating models for cities, as opposed to looking to increase the efficiency of decadent urban models, which only serves to draw out their obsolescence. Technology always requires more of an objective than simple application.

EFFICIENCY IN THE CITY

It seems unbelievable when, in a central location in a dense European, American or Asian city, we look at the intensity and the accumulation of effort and intentions on the part of human beings over the course of generations, toward creating "the street".

The street, as a place where the doors and windows lead that contain thousands of lives and individual stories about people who have decided to live together in a community, is a social miracle and an example of efficiency. The dense city is a paradigm for the desire to coexist peacefully. But they are also an example of energetic efficiency and the conservation of resources.

Historically, cities were consolidated for defensive reasons. From the standpoint of defense, living in a compact territory is much more practical, because there are fewer physical limits that need to be defended. In Europe, every civilization (Roman, Muslim, Christian) created their own walls in keeping with the territory they were capable of managing. Cities had to guarantee a supply of water, by way of wells in most cases, and provide for the constant storage of supplies.

North American cities could be conceived of as expansive, because there were no enemies to attack them. However, the United States is home to one of the best examples of high-density compact urbanity: Manhattan, where the streets are home to a huge quantity of commercial, cultural and social activities. It is a magnificent example of high-density urbanity that could have been used as a model for many newly built cities in Asia if the mechanisms for city-building, which are closely tied in with civil society, had been the same.

A compact city, where the inhabitants move through intermediate public space, the street, implies the use of less time and energy to get from one place to another. The provision of resources, such as water or energetic infrastructures, is more efficient because there is less distance to be covered. Adjacent buildings in cities, separated by party walls, have fewer exposed façades, which means less energy loss.

Compact cities are a miracle of human creation that demand governing systems to promote and support them.

Like a node in the territory, they have always had a fundamental function related to commerce. The first cities were built up around the surpluses from agricultural production. It is much more efficient for hundreds of people looking to sell their products to meet in one place in the territory, the marketplace, than for all of those people to visit hundreds of places to carry out their trade. And the city is also a territory for adding value to production processes. The guilds created in European cities in the middle ages or current technological clusters are the product of the accumulation of knowledge in a reduced physical space which allowed for the acceleration of the development of technology and knowledge.

Cities are spaces for the mediation of interests.

The beginning of the 20th century was one of the most tumultuous periods in history. There were enormously important social and political changes, and there was optimism surrounding a mechanical future where the planet's limited resources and human beings' affect on the planet were not on the agenda. After decades of experiences, and with the quadrupling of the world's population (from 1.86 billion in 1920 to 6.91 billion in 2010), the global operating system has collapsed.

The modern city, extolled by the Bauhaus school or by architects like Le Corbusier[29], is none other than the fruit of optimism in the machine era. *The functional city,*[30] where different uses were segregated within the territory, responds to a mechanicist structure as opposed to the natural order of things.

The ecosystems that survive are the ones that manage to carry out the most functions with the least consumption of energy. So it is, that lions leave near zebras, who live near large pastures where water is available, and where different species of trees grow that contain insects that also carry out different functions, as the part of a universal whole.

Aside from functionally segregating cities, modern urban design also proposed open construction. A construction in which buildings were separated by generic public space, or occupied by segregated circulation areas, highways, or by generic green areas, understood as the space outside of the functional nodes where life takes place.

All of that world developed as a result of the mass production of the automobile, which later resulted in the expansion of American and European cities, with the development of new typologies for commerce, workplaces, and production. We now recognize that the "deconstruction" of the city over a vast territory is a very inefficient model that requires a large quantity of energy and resources in order to function.

The connected self-sufficient city is based on the regeneration of territories that have already been built. It is impossible to imagine that many of the buildings in urban areas in Europe and America that have found to be inefficient could be torn down. The loss of energy implied in destroying things that have already been built, which also required a significant use of energy in the first place, as well as the important investments that would be required to build entire new neighborhoods are reasons behind the remodeling of cities. Cities have always been built on top of themselves.

The urban layouts defined by the transportation system in a city like Phoenix, one of the biggest suburban structure in the world, could be densified perfectly well to support a compact city without requiring fundamental transformations in current property structures. In fact, many city centers today are nothing more than the accumulation of cycles of functional densification, conserving the layout of the streets and augmenting the built volume.

Many American cities should probably begin the densification and recycling process if they wish to improve their efficiency and reduce their energetic dependence. It will be a historic phenomenon.

Compact cities have public space structures with a great capacity for adaptation, that can be used as the foundation for functional and productive reforms. The center of Taipei is a magnificent example, combining large avenues that define superblocks with smaller-scaled roads that connect landscapes built of low buildings that house markets after dark.

Sao Paulo is a paradigmatic case of a city organized along streets that could very well belong to an American suburb. However, twenty and thirty-story buildings, with varying degrees of density, are lined up along the homogenous net of streets, mixed throughout the city with old two-story villas, which serve as meeting places, housing restaurants or businesses. Between a city center full of skyscrapers and a periphery structured into *favelas*, there are large portions of the city that intelligently mix together two-story and twenty-story buildings, and which are great examples of urbanity, though they do not have a traditional urban form. Bombay is based on an urban layout inspired in many areas by British urban culture, as well as a number of Chinese cities. Its boundless growth into a megalopolis requires a structural meditation on the typology of the new suburban neighborhoods and the quality of the public space that they create.

Many of these neighborhoods in Asia have produced a new type of city that could respond to the standard of territories with little identity, similar to Eastern European cities after the war, but with thirty-five story buildings. Single developments with 10,000 units and a density like New York, but without the urban structure of its streets or the functional diversity of its offices and business that make it into a city.

Many European cities are familiar with the problems associated with this kind of urban development, for example in the French *banlieues*. They provide a short-term solution to the question of providing housing to respond to waves of immigration, but they lack the urban spatial and social regulations which make human beings into citizens.

When we analyze many of the new urban structures being built in Asia, we can understand their fundamental obsolescence, because as opposed to being based on new principles, they are too often based on an idea of a resource-consuming progress that is no longer feasible in our world.

VELOCITY IN THE CITY

For all of those reasons, we need to propose new models for structuring the new cities that will be built in coming year, for rehabilitating compact European cities and for restructuring the megalopolises that emerge in the world at large.

Every city admits certain functions located in specific places, based on their economic and social activities, which should operate in a particular way. Public space, according to the current model of five networks that structure the operations of cities, is the space that manages people's mobility in a city. But it is much more than an infrastructure where fluids or vehicles can circulate. It is a space for social interaction, for meetings and for the representation of the social phenomenon.

The fundamental element that defines urban space is its "velocity". In physics, velocity is a factor that relates space and time. The world moved at the velocity of a horse for centuries, during which agriculture was the essential activity. Beginning in the 19th century, it moved at the velocity of a train, which allowed for conquering territories and structuring new cities that ended up consolidating urban metro systems beginning in the early 20th century. From the nineteen fifties on, cities have been moving at the velocity of the automobile, which defines whether something is near or far as a part of the daily human habitat. Cities that were designed in the age of equine mobility are now able to support mechanical mobility in exchange for losing space dedicated to social interaction.

In the Internet age, the world moves at the velocity of interactions with information that is distributed by networks and is generated in offices and homes and, more recently, by individuals in movement across the planet at the velocity of the information they are generating at the same time.

As we said before: Internet has changed the way we life, but it has yet to alter the physical space in which we live. What kind of urban velocity corresponds to the information society?

The information society transforms how we relate with the rest of the world by introducing time as a factor in the management of our interaction with others. Telework or distance education does not only allow for deferring tasks in space, but also in time.

Time is an essential material in our life project.

In the information society, we live simultaneously in different spaces and times.

The networked society allows for simultaneously building a high-speed global system and a low-speed local one.

The cities of the future have to be made up of neighborhoods with high environmental and functional quality, in close proximity to housing and the areas where people live, connected globally in real time to information networks. Cities where people can walk or take public transportation to work and shop for basic necessities nearby, with habitable public space and neighborhood communities, and where schools and businesses are integrated into the urban framework. At the same time, they need to have effective metropolitan transportation systems, to connect neighborhoods and which provide access to airports and high-speed trains. Cities that are connected to the world through information networks that are accessible from any point in the city, as one more aspect of public space. Therefore, basic free access to the Internet through Wi-Fi networks in public space is equivalent to the public space of the street. Can we imagine a city where people would have to pay to use the streets? Information systems are already a part of the basic systems for urban mobility, for public transportation, for access to businesses and for social interaction.

The cities of the futures should be built by putting together the best of "smart" and "slow" environments.
Many slow cities inside one smart city.

A STREET IS NOT A HIGHWAY

In Barcelona's Eixample, Ildefons Cerdà was ahead of his time; he structured the network of roads in keeping with a comprehensive mobility to which cities were not yet subject at the time. The streets were divided into areas for vehicles, areas for pedestrians, and spaces where urban structures could be installed to provide services in public space. Green areas between roads were places to pass the time. As such, the "square", the urban meeting place according to urban models in the 18th and 19th centuries, does not exist in the extensions carried out after the walls were torn down in European cities. They don't exist in New York either. Times Square is more of a large-scale intersection in the shape of a medieval city than a nineteenth-century-style square.

The development of the automobile industry allowed for the emergence of sprawl, uncontrolled urban expansion, in American cities, and promoted a lifestyle at the speed of a car, which led to important transformations.

The construction of highways inside cities is another of the phenomena that indicate how cities have developed.

During the 1950s, owning a car and circulating freely throughout the territory was a symbol of social and economic progress. In fact, transportation engineers had a great deal of influence on how cities were organized. During those years, there were also plans to build a highway on Fifth Avenue in New York. The geographer Jane Jacobs[31], among others, initiated a popular movement that finally prevented its construction. In the city of Valencia in the 1960s, there were plans to build a highway in the former bed of the Turia river, to improve traffic in the city. A significant popular movement halted the initiative, and years later the riverbed was transformed into a 15-kilometer-long park that houses a wide variety of cultural and social infrastructures for the city.

However, high-speed roadways and elevated highways were built inside many other cities. All of these phenomena take place in the context of industrial development, which emphasizes productivity, mobility and a version of the city and the country centered on development. Barcelona also took up many of these infrastructures, as have a large number of cities all over the world.

More traffic means, without a doubt, more collapse of public space. At any rate, the construction of perimeter ring roads in European cities, beginning in the nineteen eighties, began to displace that collapse toward the periphery. That period was also when the refurbishment of Paris's Champs Elysées was carried out, where, for the first time, a large urban avenue in a big European city reduced the space dedicated to vehicle traffic and increased the width of the sidewalks. This phenomenon of reclaiming urban public space has coincided with the demolition of elevated roadways inside cities.

PUBLIC SPACE IN TAIWAN

In 2003, we participated in an international competition in Taiwan for the urban waterfront in the city of Keelung[20], a port city about 20 kilometers away from the capital of Taipei, and our entry won. City squares, as places for social interaction, did not exist there. There were only the "night markets" that are put up and taken down each day, a primitive expression of the role of cities as nodes for commerce. The highway that connects the city of Taipei with the seventh busiest port in the world, in terms of container

traffic, passes, literally, right through the center of the city, and
it is built on top of another elevated roadway that, in turn, sits atop
the old riverbed.

For all of those reasons, an agreement had been reached with the port
to occupy part of the inner harbor to create an open public space, or
more than a hectare, since the urban center, between the train station
and city hall, is occupied by a busy, heavily transited road.

Our project proposed the construction of a platform that ended
in a large-scale wooden surface, containing a number of urban
elements, which was quickly occupied by the city's inhabitants and
taken over as their own.

That competition is a good example of the creation of a central
public space for a city and a country that, in the wake of an
important quantitative development, is now faced with developing
qualitatively as well. Architecture and design, in these cases, as
has been the case in China and is currently the case in India, are
indicators of the consolidation of progress, represented by public
space in cities.

REDUCING MANDATORY MOBILITY

A city that tends toward self-sufficiency should minimize
the energy consumed for mobility in public space, especially
mandatory mobility. We should move more information and less
people and things in the world. Implementing intelligent mobility,
which saves energy in cities, is not only a question of using sensors
that allow for better traffic regulation or installing networked
navigators in automobiles. In order for a city to consume less
energy, there needs to be a reduction in the mandatory mobility
that forces thousands of people to travel from one side of the city to
the other to get to work.

Mandatory mobility in cities with metro systems, city buses and trams implies heavy energy consumption associated with public transportation. In Barcelona, 24% of the energy consumed is used for transportation. 95% of this consumption is satisfied by petroleum derivatives. Likewise, daily travel through the city to go to work takes up an average of one hour per person. If it is evaluated in relation to productivity, this fact represents a significant quantity in economic terms, calculated as 3.5% of Spain's GDP in a study by *La Caixa*[32].

In mixed neighborhoods, where people both live and work, if 50% of people lived and worked in the same neighborhood it would create significant savings in energy and time.

As such, industrial neighborhoods inside cities, where people work during the day, but which are empty at night, and residential neighborhoods, especially on the outskirts, which are deserted during that day, yet are full of vital energy at night, are the first candidates to be remodeled in order to allow for functional hybridization.

In a society of entrepreneurs, the workspaces are places with the best access to the network and the nicest ambient conditions. In the 1980s and 90s, the idea of telecommuting was introduced as a way of saving energy and improving people's quality of life. A large number of companies, especially in America, where commuting distances are larger, began to encourage people to work remotely from home, at least partially.

In the study called "Telework and Telecenters as a Factor in Territorial Equilibrium" ["El teletrabajo y los telecentros como factor de reequilibrio territorial"] we studied how many professions could be carried out remotely, either totally or partially, using a network, and which transversal resources could be implemented in new places where work via networks could be done, outside of the companies themselves. We confirmed that more than 40% of jobs in Europe could be networked, which would imply creating new mechanisms for work and study that do not require daily personal contact with co-workers or fellow students.

Seen in another light, if 50% of the population could work from home, , or in a resource center near home, two days a week, it would eliminate 20% of the mandatory mobility in the city.

Reeducation concerning mandatory mobility also implies reducing the investment in public transportation or dedicating that investment to renovating transportation systems to make them more sufficient and ecological.

The accumulation of different solutions intended to foment working near home is one of the fundamental goals of self-sufficient cities. An understanding of the city as a network of slow, self-sufficient neighborhoods where people live, work and rest, would reduce overall mandatory mobility in the city.

Throughout the 20th century, we have watched the density of vehicular traffic steadily increase in cities. The key to its transformation lies in giving people back the time that cities and the lifestyle we have created steals from them. The most fortunate among us can decide how and where they want to work, in relation to their homes and their interests.

HEALTHY CITIES

Likewise, public space is responsible for creating differentiated ambient qualities in front of each of the buildings where inhabitants reside.

Cerdà drew a street in front of each building in the Eixample, which was connected to any other place in the city, but in the interior of the city blocks, he also drew a green space to transfer clean healthy air directly to the buildings' windows. It is a well-known story. When streets were built for mobility, green spaces were eliminated to create greater urban density and to increase productivity.

One of the important projects in coming decades will involve taking over more public space for cities, with more green spaces around buildings, more efficiency in both public and private mobility systems, and reduced levels of mandatory mobility.

If cities are not healthy, they are not cities.

The convergence of interests between public health and the city is more important every day. A number of illnesses, associated especially with the respiratory system, have emerged as a result of the urban systems created for inhabiting the territory. Investing in quality public space, with green areas and temperatures and humidity levels appropriate to urban space, will allow for the reduction of urban heat islands and, as a result, a decrease in the illnesses caused by overheated and contaminated urban environments.

There are already programs in place at a number of universities to study the impact of urban design on public health, as well as its potential for improving the quality of life of people who live in cities.

The urban habitat has to foster human life.

The materials used in building the city are also responsible for the quality of life.

Cities and buildings, as accumulators of material, can act as urban ecosystems created with healthful materials, or they can be places where a large amount of unhealthful chemicals are accumulated, which, in direct contact with people, can represent serious problems for human health in the long and short term.

If the enlargements of cities that were carried out in the 19th century in order to improve people's living conditions, urban regeneration in the 21st century should be associated with the introduction of materials and live cycles in urban products that are compatible with human life.

LARGE AVENUES

As we have said before, cities should be able to operate at, at least, two different speeds. If people worked closer to their homes, it would eliminate part of the private traffic inside the city, and on the neighborhood scale, pedestrian zones could be enlarged, as well as the urban space dedicated to movement by bicycle.

On an urban scale, high-speed public transportation systems should be developed with the idea of providing better urban mobility at a lower cost, with a reduced environmental impact and as little occupation of public space as possible.

In order for that to be possible, solutions can be implemented both in the transportation system and in how it is integrated into the city. In the 1960s, the mayor of Curitiba (Brazil), Jaime Lerner, an architect, urban planner and author of the book *Urban Acupuncture*[33], introduced the "metronization of the bus system". His idea was that the city should be transformed quickly and with as little investment as possible. He developed a system that took advantage of the city's broad avenues, using large bi-articulated buses that circulated in exclusive bus lanes, and where people were expected to buy their tickets at stations located in public space, as opposed to on board the buses. The model was exported to Mexico, with the Metrobus, to Colombia, with the Transmilenio, and to the rest of Latin America.

In Europe, cities have promoted the development of metro lines, which require enormous investments. A metro line costs between 70 and 95 million euros per kilometer, compared with 12-16 million euros/km. for a tram (more, if there are tunnels) or 50,000 euros/km. for a city bus. Trams have been reintroduced in a number of European cities over the past few years. They have the advantage of running on electricity. There are also disadvantages, however: they are very invasive, they require a transformation of public space with overhead cables and ground structures, and they are associated with a protection system that belongs more to the 19th century than the 21st. When city buses run on electricity (which will happen soon), will the bulky and inflexible infrastructures associated with trams really make sense?

REENGINEERING URBAN MOBILITY
Another strategy to develop is rethinking the layout of transportation systems which, in the case of city buses, can be transformed from one day to the next.
Barcelona's Agency of Urban Ecology, in conjunction with Barcelona's public transportation operator (TMB) carried out a proposal for the transformation of the city bus system. The proposal is simple: since Barcelona has a system of roads based on an orthogonal grid, why not create city bus lines that run on a single street, either vertically (between the sea and the mountain) or horizontally (between the Llobregat and Besòs rivers), every three blocks?
The current layout of city bus routes responds to historic inertia and a series of circumstantial decisions that have become obsolete with respect to the evolution of the demand for mobility in the city and the construction of new transportation infrastructures. It's like a plate of spaghetti stretched out on top of a map of the city where,

in some cases, there are as many as five bus lines running on the same street. It is easy to understand that the use of city buses in Barcelona has been declining steadily over the years. Taking a bus in the city is practically impossible, except for habitual users, because the layout of the bus lines is completely irrational and incomprehensible for most of the city's inhabitants. The proposal for an orthogonal reorganization of the network of city buses operates under the condition of transferring between buses in order to move diagonally. This reorganization of the network means that more than 50% of bus riders will gain five minutes per ride, whereas only 10% will need to add a few minutes to their trips. Add to that the number of new riders who will be picked up once there is no longer a need for previous knowledge of the route before hopping on a bus. With this proposal, you only need to remember that you can always find a bus stop within no more than 300 meters from any spot in the city, and from there you can get anywhere, making a maximum of one transfer, riding along horizontal and vertical streets. The new network has 26 lines, as opposed to upwards of 80. The idea is to enlarge the Eixample. Extending the initiative that was intended to homogenize the services in the city for all inhabitants, on the level of public transportation, with as little cost as possible, making the city easy to understand.

Cerdà's design for the enlarged intersections is ideal for installing bus stops where the lines cross one another. In fact, this system serves to confirm the subtlety of Cerdà's project. According to Salvador Rueda, the fact that every three streets there is one wider street, allows for the creation of "superblocks"[3] about 400 meters long. This could promote the creation of pedestrian zones in the interior of these superblocks, where means of mechanical mobility would be reduced.

Likewise, this change in the model would imply alterations to the large avenues that cross the city, creating a diagonal route from one ring road to the next. The Diagonal, Parallel and Meridiana Avenues would become civic and pedestrian axes, as opposed to housing large volumes of traffic. Beyond the questions of mobility that each of those roads is attended to address, according to the technical studies, it would also be interesting to promote the role they play as points of reference within the city.

In 2010, Josep Bohigas, along with a number of other people, promoted a project to transform the Paral·lel into a macro-event for one weekend. At the beginning of the twentieth century, the street was a major center for leisure with cafés and cabarets lined up along a pedestrian thoroughfare. The initiative transformed the historic street, making it the setting for sporting events, festivals, concerts, fairs and other events that reclaimed the civic nature of the space. Traffic-cone urban design, he called it: as opposed to making major changes to urban space, a few simple plastic cones allow for cutting off traffic, allowing for inhabitants of the city to take over public space and functionally transforming the city instantly without the need for any kind of investment.

More and more, cities are introducing this kind of instantaneous, temporary appropriation of public space for a use that extends beyond mobility and commerce.

Introducing time as a functional variable in cities.

Every large avenue in any city can be transformed, using new rules, with a functional and social program that reinforces its role as an interface for urbanity.

Testing the city allows for socializing its potential for change.

SHORTENING THE TIME FOR FINDING PARKING IN THE CITY.
Another of the objectives in limiting the use of energy for mobility
involves reducing the time that automobiles spend in public space.
Reducing the number of automobiles in the city would increase the
ease of movement. Another improvement would involve shortening
the amount of time people spend looking for a place to park.
Information technologies can provide a solution to that problem.
In fact, today automobiles can be equipped with a navigator as a
standard feature. The newest cell phones have GPS trackers and
navigation systems built in. Current systems allow for mapping out
destinations in a city, but they provide very little information about
where to park in public space. Sensors associated to each space in
collective parking lots would save up to ten minutes of the time it
takes to find parking.

There are different international initiatives directed at creating a
system that allows for installing sensors in every parking space in
the city. That way, drivers can use their navigation systems to find
out where there are available spaces so that they can head directly
to a free space. The systems employed are magnetic, optical or a
combination of both.

In recent years, Barcelona has implemented what are called
green zones (parking areas for residents) and blue zones. They
are all metered spaces, as a way of promoting the use of public
transportation, while they also increase municipal revenue that can
be invested in the management and maintenance of public space.
In fact, cars have ample information about the city, but the city
hardly knows anything about the vehicles that circulate there, or
where they are headed. In the entrances to Barcelona, on Sunday
afternoons, traffic circulates in the opposite direction in at least
one of the lanes leading out, in order to increase the capacity for

vehicular traffic entering the city. If the city knew where all the vehicles were going, it could reprogram the directions of the streets and the lengths of the traffic light cycles. That would promote greater fluidity in mobility, reducing circulation times for vehicles and, as a result, their energy consumption. This strategy to improve the flow of traffic in cities will be implemented in coming years following the initiatives tied in with "smart cities".

Traffic lights and the direction of circulation on city street will be incorporated, in the near future, into navigators in automobiles and smart phones, which will allow for drivers to choose the correct route at any given time to reach their destinations more quickly.

PAY-PER-USE STREETS

Another strategy developed in recent year, in cities like London or Stockholm, involves controlling traffic in city centers using a toll system that recognizes license plates and the idea of pay-per-use. In the "age of access", as described by Jeremy Rifkin, the use of things is much more important than ownership. However, the paradoxical situation could arise in which inhabitants would be asked to pay to use public space in city centers, like in a theme park.

That kind of solution only favors people with more economic resources. If we compare the use of public space with Internet use, one of the principles that has worked in information networks from the beginning is neutrality. You can't make information circulate faster on the Internet, even if you pay for it. In fact, in cities such as Paris, Minneapolis or Miami, Internet access is free in public space. It would be more logical to reward people who make more efficient use of public transportation.

In Los Angeles and other American cities, there are traffic lanes on freeways that can only be used by cars carrying two or more people.

There is a growing tendency to personalize urban mobility according to vehicle type, time of day, the number of people travelling or the area of the city. All of that should not be in detriment to the freedom to use public space; those who use it most efficiently should be rewarded.

THE CREATION OF URBAN MOBILITY STANDARDS
Cities and the entities that govern them should promote progress in urban systems, as opposed to acting as mere consumers of what the market offers them.
What kind of leadership do cities exercise with respect to the solutions that operate within those cities?
Local governments should fix standards in which they define their ambitions for the management of public space and their infrastructure networks. From a functional point of view, it is one of the fundamental missions of public managers.
Let's imagine that a city decides that only vehicles with specific characteristics can circulate in the city center. For example, only electric vehicles, or ones that can hold two people, or those that occupy a maximum of 1.7 meters when parked in public space (which allows for parking the perpendicular to the road, with current widths). Then the industry would be forced to respond to the requirements of those cities, which would finally be direct motors of technological innovation.
Jaime Lerner moved in that direction when he decided to install bi-articulated buses in Curitiba's public transportation system, in collaboration with Volvo. That solution was taken up by other cities. On the other hand, a number of city councils have implemented bicycle-sharing systems that only operate in their own cities. And we are beginning to see car-sharing with electric cars.

There are latent economic potentials in cities that should be developed to provide services to inhabitants, based on the sustainability of public finances and the evolution of the systems in keeping with technological developments. Creating city consortiums would be useful, to exert a direct influence on industry, to talk about what kind of mobility should be promoted. Defining a code of elements that are compatible with the city. A system that defines what kind of vehicles, motorcycles or bicycles should be used. And that is a process that can generate economy for cities that take the lead in taking innovative decisions for their own operations.

THE URBAN OPERATING SYSTEM

The creation of standards for cities in the information society should bring with it the creation of an urban operating system that allows for the different networks and systems to be connected. While societies in every period have used the technologies available to them to transform cities, to make them more efficient and to promote human well-being, now the connected self-sufficient city promotes the local production of resources and decreased energetic consumption on every scale. Michael Weinstock, of London's Architectural Association asserts that every civilization surpasses its predecessor by using less energy and managing more information.

The possibility that new technologies could dissolve into the city, by way of small sensors connected with one another, would allow for increasing the efficiency of urban networks by providing information about the city.

The so-called Internet of things allows for capturing constant data about what is happening in the city and obtaining real-time information on parameters related to its operation: traffic, people gathering in specific areas, water stress in urban green areas, the accumulation of waste material garbage bins, the lighting needs in different places and at different time, the concentration of contaminants in the air, etc.

The city, as a system, operates with service networks that allow it to function based on protocols that are implemented in those networks. In most cases, the networks work in parallel, without taking advantage of the potential synergies between them. Many cities, like many governments, understand governance as a sectorial activity where the departments work as hermetic systems that don't allow for the exchange of information. In coming years programs should be deployed to obtain information about how cities work, to make them transparent, and to look for ways of increasing the effectiveness of the systems. That could lead to the development of an urban operating system as the support for better efficiency and better management of current urban services.

Santa &Cole is a design publishing company created in Barcelona in 1985, a year before Barcelona's candidacy for the Olympics was accepted.

The business model inspired by literary publishing is, in fact, very different from the traditional companies that produce design material, specialized in the technologies associated with the machines they use. In that case, the technical knowledge, sometimes coming down from a family traditions, leads to a particular product (wood casting, or metal casting, or any other kind). Santa & Cole, as a publisher, could work with any manufacturer. What is important is the intellectual property associated with the design. During the Olympic years, they developed a number of urban elements that are now an inherent part of the image of public space in Barcelona, associated with some of the best designers in the city. Javier Nieto, the company's president, asserted that when any city or company in the world acquires one of their pieces, the actually take in a part of Barcelona's urban culture. They incorporate in interest for the construction of public space as a place for coexistence among citizens. In 2002, they set up their forestry division, with the aim of lending more systemic characteristic to their construction of public space. That way they could encompass from furniture and lighting to landscaping, all of it "edited" based on quality principles.

In 2006, in conjunction with the Universitat Politècnica de Catalunya (UPC), they created the company Urbiótica, which works developing an operating system to make cities more efficient. Domotics for the city.

The construction of new cities, or new neighborhoods, can be undertaken using new paradigms related to the organization of a functional structure that can incorporate more efficient urban systems. However, the biggest current challenge lies in transforming, existing cities, which are home to more than three billion people, to make them more efficient.

In order to make cities more efficient, we need to increase the resolution of the information we have about them.

In coming years, cities will need to begin a process of re-information. Using sensors installed in the city itself, real-time information can be collected on mobility, waste materials, air quality and other aspects. Based on investments that will finance themselves, it will improve the management of public services. The information society is oriented toward services, not products. A good example is urban lighting. Cities today buy streetlights and pay invoices billed for kilowatts and maintenance. It would be smarter to consider holding competitions to award contracts based on lumens or light quality, which are the services that are needed in city streets and squares. An efficient and intelligent system that combines design, quality and characteristics of public lighting.

THE OPEN DATA CITY

If cities produce information, and we can obtain it and organize it, who should control that information?

The information is tied in with the city government.

During the 20th century, we witnessed the consolidation of democratic systems, where all kinds of people in different social situations have been able to participate in elections for national parliaments and mayor's offices.

Of the seven billion people on the planet, 75% of them live in the 115 countries that use democratic systems.

The development of global information networks, however, has the potential to change governing systems.

Information is one of the raw materials in managing how communities are governed. Traditionally, it has been concealed in order to control society, in the same way that companies would hide key information and protect their data in order to maintain their positions in the market.

However, in recent years we have witnessed a number of initiatives related to open code and open systems, which mean that citizens can interact and participate in the design of the products that they use.

As such, platforms for Open City Data have begun to emerge, which propose making the information emerging from the city transparent, so that both governments and citizens can use that knowledge to improve their quality of life.

Making the information transparent and making rational decisions about the management of cities, with the knowledge of the inhabitants, will be one of the rules of governance in the 21st century.

In order to make the data comprehensible, visualization systems will need to be developed to foment understanding of what is being analyzed. The process, therefore, that should be promoted involves rehumanizing politics, the management of the *polis*, by making transparent the rules and the decisions concerning the management of the city.

Politics defines the protocols for the exchange of information in cities. Governments must first write the operating system, the protocols and the applications which will generate the content that will be developed in the city.

Making democracy into a regular activity, where citizens participate in a more direct manner, with adequate information, is part of the new management protocols that cities can take on, with the aim of involving their inhabitants in the decisions that are made.

6. City
(1.000.000)

Cities are informed energy.
Systems of functional, social, and governing structure developed
over centuries by their inhabitants in order to support human life.
Cities are accumulators of material energy. An aggregation of
buildings and urban structures that have required enormous
amounts of human, physical and economic resources to exist.
They are also accumulators of human energy. The concentrate
social and intellectual activities that belong to a culture in which
people, families, organizations and business come together to
satisfy their needs as living beings.
A city is an ecosystem where a community of citizens interacts
with a physical structure in a permanent exchange of material and
energy aimed at improving human life.
Finally, cities are cultural constructions. They represent the
aspirations of a consolidated community through a shared idea.
A place to educate people and exchange knowledge. A place for
creativity.

A CITY'S KNOW-HOW
Cities, like organizations, have their own know-how. They know
why they are the way they are. They are the most efficient response
to the environmental needs, functional needs and the need for
obtaining resources that brought them into existence.
In two similar-sized cities, with the same number of dwellings and
the same cubic meters of buildings, the shape of each city will be
defined by the processes that have informed their growth. And that
process will be affected by the environment in which the city is

housed and the culture that provides it with its character.

Cities, like living beings, have been subject to natural selection. Cities that, in the middle ages, were the economic centers of their countries are now the capitals of tiny provinces, because their geographical standing and their economic leadership no longer lends them importance. And other cities and regions in the world emerge with renewed force, because they possess the necessary resources, material or human, to gain competitiveness.

The shape of a city doesn't define it.

If a portion of Barcelona's Eixample were copied and built in any other city in the world, its shape would not result in the same kind of interaction that takes place in that part of Barcelona. Cities are an accumulation of incidents, events, memories, relationships, of economy, culture, and an intransferable genealogy. That is their "know-how".

If cities are informed energy, it is their metabolism that allows them to function. However, cities at the beginning of the 21st century have a by default metabolism. They have been built based on the accumulation of layers of independent systems that responded to a coherence that was characteristic of an industrial economy. The concentration of external production systems that pour their resources into the city, as a system that consumes a lot and generates very little.

The city transforms the resources that come from nature into urban detritus.

THE URBAN CLOCK. THE AGE OF CITIES.

Cities are physical x-rays of their economic and social history. The shape of the city follows the shape of its economy, built up on the action of the political, cultural and social structures from each period.

At the beginning of the 21stcentury, the planet is home to aborigine habitats among remote Amazon tribes or in sub-Saharan Africa, nomadic peoples in the Mongolian steppe, medieval social structures in Afghanistan, regions undergoing the industrialization process in Asia and tertiary economies in the United States. Cities have an urban clock which demonstrates their state of development with respect to the social, economic and cultural structures under which they operate. And cities show us the physical traces of this temporary condition of techno-economic development in a nearly immediate way.

Nearly all known urban phenomena have developed in response to a social, cultural and economic need. We could outline a global history of urban phenomena that initiated in specific cities, in particular moment, as concrete responses to phenomena that were taking place in that city. It the situation in question generates leadership, it is later accepted and imitated on a near global level. In any case, cities have different physical and cultural characteristics, which means that some of those developments are not reproduced literally. In addition, the phenomena occur at different velocities in different cities.

Many of these developments are linked with specific technologies. The development of heavy artillery and the railroad was fundamental for the demolition of city walls in Europe in the 19th century. The elevator brought about the development of high-rise buildings, with an important initial impulse in Chicago at the end of the 19th century, and later in New York in the nineteen twenties. The development of the automobile industry allowed for the emergence of sprawl, uncontrolled urban expansion, in American cities, and promoted a lifestyle at the speed of a car, which led to important transformations in the human habitat on the periphery of cities.

The phenomena of outsourcing, often associated with global mobility, are always related with the transformation of airports which, in turn, need high-volume road that allow for connecting them with the city. Modern airports use fingers to increase the speed of boarding and disembarking. An airport without fingers demonstrates either the small size of the city where it is located, or a lack of tertiary or touristic development in the city. A highway from the airport into the city, for example, is one of the major infrastructure developed by cities that are planning to host the Olympic Games, like Barcelona did. Later, tertiary areas associated with logistics are developed in the space between the city and the airport, and then as a result, the fairgrounds (or convention centers) appear, as was the case in Barcelona and Madrid, for example. A large number of the patterns in Iran in 2010 could be found in Spain in the 1970s. An economy with few ties to the exterior, with very little tertiary activity, with a political and cultural blockade from the exterior, promotes a type of economy that tends toward self-sufficiency, with a high level of internal industrial production.

THE OLYMPIC GAMES

The Olympic Games are part of urban culture from the 20th and 21st century as an extreme form of urban marketing. If we analyze the cities that have hosted the Games, especially since the Second World War, we will observe a great intelligence in the decision process, capable of recognizing the emergence of countries and territories on a planetary scale, or even countries that exercise political and economic centrality.

In Asia, the pattern for the organization of the Olympic Games indicates a movement toward the east. In 1964, Tokyo hosted the Games at a moment when Japan's economy was developing, which helped the world get to know a developing country with abundant technological production and companies that quickly became global players. Twenty-four years later, Seoul was the Olympic capital at a moment of strength among the Asian tigers (Korea, Taiwan, Singapore and Hong Kong) that were taking up part of the basic activities that had previously been housed in Japan and were developing companies such as Samsung, Kia and others. Twenty years later, it was Beijing's turn; they organized the impressive 2008 Olympics, which showed the best of a country that is in the middle of a process of transformation.

The selection of Brazil for 2016 responds to this logic of moving the games toward areas with emerging economies. It was the same with the FIFA World Cup in South Africa in 2010. The selection of Qatar for that same competition recognizes of the emergence of the Gulf states (as a result of the gift of nature in the form of oil), which are carrying out important urban transformations by taking advantage of historic geopolitical circumstances linked with the oil economy. Beginning in the nineteen eighties, Barcelona began one of the most intense urban renovation processes in the world, creating what would come to be known as the "Barcelona model", widely publicized in recent years. The model proposes a pact among the inhabitants for the transformation of the city, in which urban space is remodeled and expanded, with quality elements, into a meeting place. Architecture plays a central role, given that economic and social progress is demonstrated physically in the city through small-scale neighborhood facilities. As such, all of the sectors of public life are included, and the participation of private initiatives in reforming the city is also promoted. With this model, there are very few architectural "icons"; rather, the idea is to promote a large number of high-quality projects that take on the city as a whole. Barcelona took on a number of strategic reforms, like the construction of the ring roads, following the Parisian model of the *boulevard périphérique* on land that had been set aside in the Master plan defined in the nineteen seventies. One of the central phenomena was opening the city up to the sea, with the transformation of obsolete industrial areas into a space for leisure activities and public use, following a process that had been implemented in cities like Boston, San Francisco or Seoul. The refurbishment of the historic port for urban uses was also part of the changes, with the participation of public and private agents. Barcelona's program worked to perfection. It is a city with a high-quality urban planning, with good buildings, and a broad architectural tradition that had been politically repressed for over forty years, with a very good Architecture school at the time, with very talented architects and a country in the midst of economic development, which saw its peak in 1992 with the Olympic Games and the Universal Expo in Seville. Barcelona took exceptional advantage of a historic opportunity, because the city had been preparing for it for years. These conditions are unlikely to be repeated in other cities in the southern or central Europe in the near future.

In fact, there are fundamental structural differences between the old, dense cities in Europe and the expansive North American cities, which are based on the "downtown/sprawl" duality, between Latin American macrocities, or the macrocities in African developing economies, the growing urbanizing process in Asia, the new cities in the Middle East, and distant Australian cities. Every place on the planet has different structural conditions that will need to undergo processes of development, regeneration or remodeling. Every city on the planet constitutes a different ecosystem, located in a different regional environment.

Therefore, determining which ingredients are operative in a city or a country is essential to understanding its potential and harnessing it to grow its economy and improve the quality of life of its inhabitants, in the long term.

ZERO EMISSIONS CITIES

Another way of evaluating cities' behavior is determining their annual CO_2 emissions. Given that food production is not taken into account in the calculations, "zero emissions" cities, or "CO_2 neutral" cities, are an achievable medium-term goal.

Masdar is the project for a district that is currently being built in Abu Dhabi. It is perhaps the first project that has set the objective of creating a "zero emissions" city.

The project, designed by Foster & Partners, takes on a series of radical decisions from the outset. The city where the district is located is designed with narrow streets following the urban tradition of desert cities, that create shade and cooling using water systems in public space and the control of air circulation. Automobiles will be electric and they will operate using a magnetic system, without a driver, like the systems for transporting containers in the world's biggest ports. There will be large parking zones on the outskirts and shuttles that will allow for changing from one transportation system to another. Energy will be produced locally, either on the roofs of buildings, or through photovoltaic parks located near the city.

The company Masdar, the driving force behind the project, has five divisions: Masdar City, Masdar Power, Masdar Capital, Masdar Carbon, y Masdar Institute. The first building constructed in the city, which is already in operation, is the Masdar Institute, a University center that works in collaboration with MIT.

Masdar Carbon, on its part, is in charge of providing the definition for Zero Emission, which can have different interpretations and is referred to using different names. It is determined by evaluating the CO_2 given off during the establishment of the city and during its operation, along with the compensatory measures undertaken.

There are three ways of evaluating the emissions:
Strictly Zero Carbon: No emissions. There can be no compensation for the carbon that might be emitted during the operation of the city.
Net Zero Carbon: All of the carbon emissions within the realm of the city are eliminated or balanced within the city itself. Balancing means compensate for accumulated emission using "carbon credits" or credits from renewable energy generated in the same network.
Carbon Neutral: All of the emissions that the city is responsible for can be managed by buying compensations from third parties out-side the city limits. In coming years, different initiatives will allow for transforming these abstract evaluations into model for real-time evaluations from within cities.

MILESTONES IN URBAN INVENTION
The history of humanity is full of projects that entail a paradigm shift, which later become models for other cities.
The first enclosed shopping center was Southdale, which opened in Edina, Minnesota, near Minneapolis, in 1956.
The first amusement park was Disneyland, designed and built under the direct supervision of Walt Disney, and opened on July 18, 1955.
The first automobile assembly line was built by Henry Ford.
In 1899, he began his own automobile manufacturing company in order to produce enough automobiles so that anyone could have one.
In 1908, in Detroit, Michigan, Ford divided the simplified tasks in-volved in the manufacture of an automobile and broke up those tasks

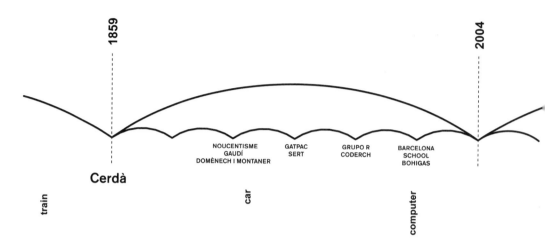

1859

2004

NOUCENTISME
GAUDÍ
DOMÈNECH I MONTANER

GATPAC
SERT

GRUPO R
CODERCH

BARCELONA
SCHOOL
BOHIGAS

Cerdà

train

car

computer

After 150 years of urban development in Barcelona, we are faced with a two-fold cyclical shift: a generational shift and a paradigm shift.

into individual functions assigned to each worker. The conception of each worker as part of an automobile manufacturing machine.
The first highway was built in Italy in 1925 to connect Milan with Lake Como. It is known as the Autostrada dei Laghi.
The first electric elevator was built by Werner von Siemens in 1880. The safety and speed of electric elevators was improved significantly by Frank Sprague. The inventor Anton Freissler developed Von Siemens's ideal and built a successful company in Austria-Hungary.
The first refurbishment of a port to make it available for public use was in Baltimore, Maryland in the nineteen seventies.
Creating self-sufficient city blocks, in self-sufficient neighborhoods, in a zero-emissions city, will establish a new paradigm that will define patterns for the regeneration and construction of cities in the 21st century.
The best way to conserve wealth is to augment it.

THE REGENERATION OF BARCELONA

Cities are built around paradigms that defend action programs that span at least a generation.

In the nineteen eighties, in the context of democratic advancement, Barcelona took on the challenge of transforming the city on a human scale and equipping it with facilities and services that had never been built previously. In the seventies, Barcelona expanded due to the economic developmentalism that led to large waves of immigration. In the twenties, the city experienced the dream of social renovation and economic process which had its zenith in the International Exposition of 1929. At the end of the 19th century, it faced the construction of the Eixample and the first industrialization of the territory.

What is the paradigm for Barcelona in the wake of the severe crisis that began in 2007? How can Barcelona consolidate its position on the map of innovative cities on a global scale? How can an economy be created based on the transformation of the city, without increasing its physical dimensions?

The next great paradigm for cities is becoming producers of resources again, as opposed to net consumers. The production of energy, goods, food and knowledge, all in order to build a city that is organized around a new urban ecology, which promotes social unity. The driving factor for this transformation is the change from a city that is basically entirely built, to a city with an annual balance of greenhouse gases that tends toward zero. Zero Emissions Barcelona. In order for this to be possible, we need to define concrete strategies on multiple scale, to guide any other decision that is made in relation to the management of the city. In that way, the construction of the city will respond to the development of a paradigm and the conquest of a vision, as opposed to the management of day-to-day problems or the development of projects that respond to circumstantial opportunities.

The Barcelona that defines its urban design in terms of forms and functions. The Barcelona that invented the concept of "urban design" can invent a new discipline oriented toward the regeneration of cities where the two fundamental vectors to be incorporated in the design are energy and information.

ZERO EMISSIONS BARCELONA

At the end of 2010, at the IAAC we decided to begin research centered on the city of Barcelona in order to define the strategies for the new Zero Emissions Barcelona.

During the research we carried out, we arrived at the conclusion that we would need to promote the development of neighborhoods that could produce a maximum of their resources locally and that would operate at a low velocity within a city that would be hyperconnected with the both, both by physical high-speed transportation systems and by information networks, and be able to generate all the energy it needed locally. Resuming this new paradigm into strategies and concrete plans results in eleven lines of action.

First, buildings and city blocks would need to be transformed into self-sufficient constructions, capable of producing energy using renewable systems, managed by intelligent networks. The first transformations would be carried out in areas that were already under transformation, like 22@, or in a number of non-central neighborhoods. Later, all of the neighborhoods in the city would need to be addressed, preserving the buildings and environments with the most heritage value, which

contribute other resources and values to the urban economy.
Second, a plan for the energetic rehabilitation of neighborhoods
would need to be promoted, encompassing building insulation
and energy conservation, especially in buildings put up during the
nineteen seventies, which have more deficient infrastructures.
This physical regeneration process should be made into a platform
for professional training, social cohesion and economic activity.

Third, more parameters would need to be added to building
qualifications, beyond their form and function. An energy
coefficient, epsilon, could locally define the relationship between
the energy produced and the energy consumed, and buildings with
better balances could be rewarded for their role in avoiding large-
scale infrastructures, and their maintenance, in the city.
The environmental and metabolic evaluation of buildings should
also incorporate factors that concern the management of the
water, the waste materials and the air quality they generate in their
surroundings, and their active position in the management of
information and knowledge on the neighborhood scale. In addition
to guaranteeing that any new construction or rehabilitation will be
carried out based on new structural principles.

Fourth, centralized heating systems should be promoted on a
neighborhood scale, based on the use of natural resources from the
areas surrounding the city, like the biomass from Collserola or the
temperature gradients in the Mediterranean, using biomass power
plants or geothermal springs. In parallel, large-scale structures, like
wind farms, should be sought out, to provide the foundation for
high-power energy generation in close proximity to the city.

Fifth, the reduction of mandatory movement in the city should be reduced by promoting the development of hybrid neighborhoods, especially in environments that are currently monofunctional.

Sixth, the implementation of electric vehicles —motorcycles, cars, vans, taxis, etc.—should be promoted, based on standards established by the city itself in collaboration with the automobile industry. As such, electric city buses should also be promoted, based on a new orthogonal grid. And, in conjunction, there should be a reduction in vehicle traffic throughout broad areas of the city.

Seventh, the reinformation of public space should be promoted with the creation of intelligent networks that integrate information generated by the city, picked up by sensors and actuators. A Service Integration Platform would allow for more efficient management of the city's systems. Which would lead to the creation of new economic models linked to the economy of "smart cities".

Eighth, the renaturalization of public space should be promoted to achieve better quality of life, better air quality and a better ambient temperature in the city and in the areas adjacent to buildings. Collserola, the sea and the rivers should influence the city with their natural networks, integrating a new urban landscape using indigenous species.

Ninth, citizens should be encouraged to participate in the management of the city based on open data networks that share the information that the city collects with respect to itself. As such, inhabitants would be able to create platforms to improve the quality of life and promote new forms of economy.

Tenth, these ideas could be developed with precision based on agreements with research centers and national or international companies to make Barcelona into an urban laboratory dedicated to implementing solutions directed at creating a city made up of productive neighborhoods that operate at a human velocity within a hyperconnected, zero-emissions metropolis.

Lastly, all of these actions should be guided by excellence in their design and execution, putting Barcelona back into a central position in the realm of architecture and urban design on an international level.
All of this will encourage a new economy of urban innovation.

THE ECONOMY OF URBAN INNOVATION

Large organizations have suffered crises throughout their history, which, if they have been correctly managed, have allowed them to progress. It is the same for cities. They are one of the organisms on the Earth with the highest capacity for survival due to their ability to transform themselves, regenerate, grow, incorporate new technologies, increase their density and produce new interior spaces. The artificiality of the city is what allows it to survive as an organism throughout history. In order for that to be possible, each new urban era carries with it an associated economic model.
In recent decades, many Western cities have lost the ability to produce goods in order to focus on the production of the cities themselves: their neighborhoods and buildings, as a fundamental part of their economy. The growth of the world's population, the globalization of the information society, the migratory waves from developing countries toward consolidated economies and the increase in life spans, has meant that cities have grown in

order to accommodate an increased population. Urbanization as economy. But in new cities, where the shopping center became the new temple, the place that lent meaning to the global industrial machine, very few things were being produced.

The economy of urban innovation is based on cities becoming productive again. Where they can again rely on industry an technology to move the production of goods to the places where they are consumed. If the distributed model of resource management, characteristic of the Interned, is applied to the urban economy, new forms of business will appear, associated with service management, as opposed to the sale of products.

The economy of urban innovation understands any transformation in the physical body of the city as an investment as opposed to an expense. As an opportunity for implementing systems that imply savings with respect to the current standards for managing cities. Whereas the economy of information focused first on increasing efficiency in the workplace, and later it was centered on social relationships and domestic environments, the next challenge involves reengineering cities. In the wake of the Internet of business and the Internet of people, now we are tackling the fusion of the physical and digital worlds through the Internet of things and, with it, the Internet of cities. Any element in a city, with the appropriate informational layer, is capable of emitting and receiving information, which allows for reprogramming the services and processes in a city in order to make them more efficient. The operating costs of a city, both with respect to public services and with respect to the expenses incurred by all inhabitants to keep their vehicles and homes running, is one of the fundamental aspects of the economy.

The investment used to increase the efficiency of the city's operations will come from the savings that the investment itself will generate. Cities will always need energy in order to operate. Producing it locally using renewable energy sources, with integrated production and storage systems will guarantee supply and price stability in the face of future global imbalances. Investing in technology and solutions for connected self-sufficiency is investing in stability.

The economy of urban innovation is creating a new sector of the economy around what are called Smart Cities. It is a new field in the economy, where companies in the technology sector, in vertical services for urban networks (information, water, materials, energy and mobility), in construction and in ecology can compete to make a place for themselves in the new formats of the service-oriented economy.

Cisco's invention of IP telephones generated more traffic on the network and created a new way of communicating information that broke with the monopoly of the traditional telephone operators, who fought tooth and nail to delay the new communication formats, first in voice communications and then in video. Future operators dealing with the new city services may emerge from an evolution of the current managers, from the alliance between companies or from the creation of new operators.

Public-private alliances will be one of the fundamental formats for the future management of cities. Decades ago, operations began that involved concessions for infrastructures, such as highways, based on the safe value represented by people's mobility in the territory. Since then, new services have appeared that have developed based on the concession format. But the real estate sector in Spain, oriented toward the sale of properties and accustomed to high profitability rates, of around twenty or thirty percent, has been reluctant to invest in rental properties. However, there are some companies tied in with public works contracts, with profits of four or five percent over the total cost (in the best case scenario), that have begun to see the concession of rental housing as a field where they can make constant profits over an extended period of time. Investing in the construction a building, then renting it out for forty years, and then returning it to the public administration, may have seemed like a miracle in an environment where everything was being bought and sold at breakneck speed. Investments in the production of energy in buildings, in installing sensors in the city, in new lighting systems and waste material collection will see returns in the medium term, based on the fixed consumption that occurs in cities. Urban efficiency is a new way of investing that has widespread social repercussions.

In any case, the transformations that can be made in cities are not only of a technological order; they also encompass the functional base of the city. An intelligent city is not a stupid city with sensors added. In the same way that we are now dealing with the reform of the basic structures of Western economies, the challenge lies in reforming cities in aspects related to their physical structure and their operations, by adding a metabolic layer that orients the city's economy toward services for its inhabitants. The business opportunity lies in staying in cities. In establishing constant interaction with the inhabitants. And in encouraging the inhabitants to become entrepreneurs in new forms of economy. We are facing a shift from a product-oriented economy to a service-oriented economy. A city where the city itself is actually a service. Where there are fewer people who own and more who manage. In that sense, we need to make services –the processes related to satisfying the basic needs of inhabitants– into a science.

At the limit, the information society allows for adding value to cities without the need for investing money, necessarily, due to the use of new kinds of cooperation among citizens, and between citizens and the Administration. By creating open, collaborative networks, where the fundamental goal is human well-being.

A CITY IS AN IDEA

A city is an idea. The interaction of all of the ideas of the city is what keeps its millions of inhabitants going on a daily basis. And, occasionally, this idea needs to be stimulated through events or paradigms that group together a whole city in a collective vision. Over the past thirty years, Barcelona has gone from becoming a global icon of urban quality to squandering part of its capital in a soulless event in 2004. The next grand event must be the regeneration of the city itself, like the construction of the Eixample was in the past.

The majority of the large-scale new generation projects, precisely centered on the ring roads, were built on the occasion of the Olympic Games. The oval-shaped ring served to structure the four Olympic areas. But it left a large part of the city's relationship with the space beyond the ring-roads unfinished.

The port is a good example. In a project he presented within the framework of the HyperCatalonia project, Willy Müller wondered why ships should have to come to shore to unload their cargo of liquids or grain. Wouldn't it be possible to build an artificial island out at sea to free up the coastline? In recent years, the port of Barcelona has built up a surface area the size of the old town, on land reclaimed from the sea. But given that is has a special legal personality (which is actually governed from Spain's capital), everything that happens in the port seems like it isn't related to the city.

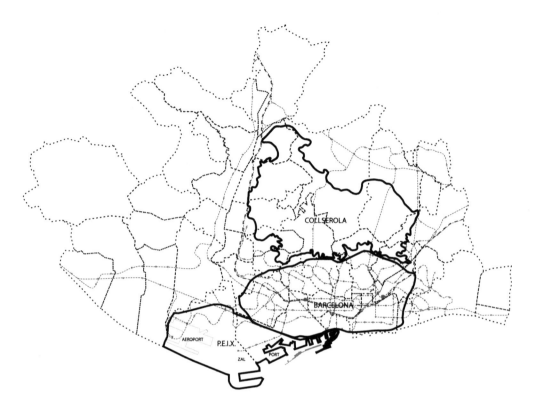

Collserola, Barcelona and the P.E.I.X. (the area that encompasses the Port, the Airport and *Zona Franca*), have similar surface areas.

In recent years, Willy Müller has been working on the transformation of the Morrot, located just a stone's throw from the monument to Columbus and at the foot of Montjuïc, in an urban area. Finally, this project, framed in the logic of the productive city, has housed a hybrid program that includes production, research, education and rental housing. The strategic vision is centered on extending the city in front of Montjuïc to connect with the new Marina del Prat Vermell neighborhood, growing out toward the Llobregat River.

A PRODUCTIVE SEAFRONT

The seafront should constitute a productive environment.
Throughout the history of port cities, the port has, in many cases,
represented those cities' largest source of income. Goods came
in through ports, which allowed for commerce; or the goods
produced locally could be exported. Fishing boats based in ports
also extracted part of the food consumed by cities, which could also
be sold in the interior. It is hard to understand how an activity as
historic as fishing is being lost in many large historic ports in big
cities, displacing this activity toward emerging territories.
The remodeling of seafronts in many big cities, like Barcelona or
Boston, has centered on promoting tourism, leisure and commerce
in the traditional spaces associated with fishing. During the
Olympic years Barcelona promoted a recreational use of the
seafront: it was a place to sunbathe, to grab a drink or to eat at a
beach bar. The pleasure of experiencing a traditional fishing port
was lost. Self-sufficient cities value and encourage productive
activities, as well as knowledge about the productivity of cities
themselves. There is no greater pleasure than watching the arrival
into port of a fishing fleet, and the unloading of the crates that they
take to the wholesale fish market where they auction their catch.
And if you're lucky, the best part is tasting some of that fish or
seafood just as it has been plucked from the sea.
Different cities on the Mediterranean coast, like Palamós, Vinaròs
or Dènia, base part of their local culture on fishing and on products
that come from the sea. The Spanish Mediterranean coast could be
described as a sequence of prawn and shrimp species of different
sizes, colors and tastes, the knowledge of which only enriches
us. This experience of local pleasure should be at the root of
globalization and our ability to move through the world.

In the 19th century, there were more than 2,740 fishing boats, merchant vessels and warships in the port of Barcelona. Now, there are only 24 fishing boats, and only one (yes, one) uses traditional fishing methods. A city that promotes self-sufficiency cannot abide the loss of knowledge, techniques or pleasures associated with the productivity of the sea.

Barcelona has also created a cluster dedicated to repairing boats, associated with maritime sports that make use of different kinds of yachts and watercraft, which have traditionally docked in the port. An industrial mechanism for sailing services.

NEW URBAN CENTRALITIES

Remodeling the seafront has been one of the most successful operations undertaken in Barcelona in recent decades. In the Middle Ages, the Mediterranean was the place where attacks and invasions could come from. That is why the large trade routes, like the Via Augusta, were built far away from the sea shore. In 19th century Barcelona, the seafront was used to build railroad infrastructures and, later, water treatment plants and power plants. The seafront was of little interest beyond port activities, or its role as a dumping ground for waste water, and it was occupied by slums during periods of intense immigration during the nineteen sixties. The Olympic Games made a large-scale operation possible for the transformation of the coastline, so that the railroad and road infrastructures were moved underground, the seafront was developed and several kilometers of urban beaches were created, which are a social success today.

This action caused the city's center of gravity to shift toward the sea. There are cities with multiple centers of gravity (like Los Angeles, for example) or cities where there is a highly defined idea about where the center is, or which is the main square, where the events with the largest political and social repercussions take place. Beijing, built as a system of rings around the Forbidden City, has Tiananmen Square.

In the case of Barcelona, its main square in the 19th century was the Plaça Sant Jaume, built above the old Roman forum. In the 20th century, the Plaça Catalunya, located between the old town and the Passeig de Gràcia has served as the main urban center.

In the 21st century, the Plaça de les Glòries will take on this role, acting as a central metropolitan square. To make this possible, the Avinguda Diagonal had to be extended down to the sea, the 22@ neighborhood, home to the city's technological companies, had to be developed, and the new Sagrera high-speed train station had to be launched. The project for the square itself is currently in development and won't be completed for at least a few years. But the shifting of a large city's center of gravity, in an ordered manner, with the aim of incorporating productive and representative elements, and 21st century infrastructures into the very heart of the city, is great news, which demonstrates the vitality of the urban context.

FROM INDUSTRIAL NEIGHBORHOODS TO HYBRID NEIGHBORHOODS

The industrial areas that exist in cities are a dysfunction that is characteristic of 20th century urban design. Neighborhoods occupied by industrial warehouses, with a high volume of heavy vehicles which sometimes emit loud noises derived from the use of machinery during business hours. Streets with very poor site development, with parking or storage spaces between the warehouses. A territory based on single-story buildings, where, in general, thousands of people arrive in private cars each day.

There is no public transportation (given the high level of dispersion) and the areas are deserted at night. They are the paradigm of a highly inefficient ecosystem.

However, in a large number of European and American cities, the reality is even worse. This low-to-the-ground monofunctional model has caught on and commercial areas have appeared that are modeled after industrial parks. Major brands dealing in food, home furnishings and technology are some of the motors behind this suburbanization of metropolitan areas in European cities.

This monofunctional system has very likely developed because it is very easy to deal with the selling a portion of land to a single agent, who is at liberty to put up a building that will only operate at certain times of day.

But, would there be a problem if housing or office buildings were built on top of those mini shopping centers or movie theaters on the outskirts of cities? Absolutely not. The commercial activities of large-scale retail establishments are perfectly compatible with those uses, because they do not generate high noise levels. The leisure activities that take place in the urban centers of many European cities are much more incompatible, when alcohol and partying transform citizens into out-of-control individuals who forget about the urban and residential character of dense cities. Industrial neighborhoods are an intermediate case, given that industrial warehouses can sometimes create noise levels that would affect the quality of life in the surroundings. Today, that problem has a technical solution through the use of soundproofing and the right kind of building design. If we consider that new types of industry or research centers are much quieter and use smaller technology, there is total compatibility.

There are some buildings in New York, built with flexible structures, on a large scale, where there is a hybridization of industrial activities, logistics, storage and lofts that serve as living spaces. Hybrid neighborhoods, where people live, work and rest, are functionally self-sufficient. A neighborhood where people can walk to work or cycle to work, results in much lower energy consumption. For all of these reasons, we are currently faced with a major project: the densification and functional hybridization of industrial parks and shopping centers in cities. The aim is to generate urban quality, to avoid a non-urban occupation of the territory and to increase the development of infrastructures. In addition, the development of green areas and public facilities on the rooftops of industrial spaces could allow for the development of new building typologies and urban typologies.

Conversely, the residential neighborhoods that were built in response to the influx of immigration in the nineteen sixties and seventies, should develop strategies to incorporate productive activities on their ground floors, in new light-weight structures, in reconverted dwellings or in newly constructed areas. The creation of workplaces in residential neighborhoods should be promoted through new centers associated with knowledge or new-generation industrial production.

PRODUCING ENERGY IN THE CITY

Energetically self-sufficient cities should reduce their energy consumption and generate energy locally. Energy will have to be produced on multiple scales and using different systems, like what happens today on a larger scale with the energy mix. In the city, energy is mainly consumed in buildings, industry, and transportation and it consists of a thermal part and an electric part. The thermal part, connected to building energy use, has to be addressed from the standpoint of building refurbishment, since buildings are largely imperfect machines in terms of maintaining heat and cold. The best systems are produced on a neighborhood or district scale through cold and heat networks that are using power plants that produce heat by burning trash or organic waste, from biogas, or using geothermal systems when the conditions underground allow for it. Electrical energy should be produced on the scale of buildings, mainly through photovoltaic systems, and using wind energy, through small- and medium-scale systems incorporated into the urban structure. Large-scale wind energy can be produced when the conditions are favorable on the geographic limits of cities, in contact with natural systems like rivers, mountains or the sea. In the case of Barcelona, the peak demand for the city is approximately 2,000 MW. Meaning, 2 GW or the power generated by two nuclear power plants. In order to produce the energy for consumption in the city, in coming years a number of regeneration plans for buildings will need to be developed to include: general retrofitting and incorporating electricity production using photovoltaic systems; creating power plants tied in with the natural systems in surrounding areas (the sea and the mountains); developing district heating and cooling networks, like Districlima, which works using the heat from burning urban waste in the Besòs plant, or the Ecoenergies network, which works using biomass and geothermal energy from underground.

If Barcelona is able to save fifty percent of the energy consumption in its buildings by increasing efficiency, it could generate all of the electricity it needs to operate by covering thirty percent of building roof space and creating distributed energy networks that incorporate storage for energy management. It would be possible due to the physical structure of the city, its density and compactness.

PROGRESS FOR CITIES

But cities don't progress individually. Any invention that appears in one city soon arrives in others. The question, then, it to define the speed at which the community of the world's cities progresses. Because today, as opposed to fierce competition among countries, which are defined by very strong political and economic barriers, there is competition among cities to attract investments, to attract companies to settle there and provide jobs for inhabitants, as well as investing in the transformation of the city. Today, cities compete to attract human capital to promote local innovation.

Cities cooperate and compete at the same time.

We live in a world of cities. Most of the world's population lives in cities. This is a phenomenon that has never before occurred in the history of humanity, and it should lead to new ways of organizing the world.

In the 19th century, the planet was governed by empires, like the British, French and Spanish empires, which extended their control by establishing colonies. The 20th century has been the century of nation-states, during which most of the member states of the United Nations were created. And the 21st century will very likely be the century of cities, a territorial translation of the distributed model for organizing the world that is characteristic of the Information Society.

Historically, economic growth was associated with the physical growth of cites, with new urban planning processes. But today, in Europe and America, cities have already been planned. As a result, we need to invent new processes so that the economy can grow without being associated with physical growth in cities.

In recent years, a number of city organizations have emerged that reflect this situation, with the aim of coordinating policies and promoting collective progress. They are platforms for debate for the purpose of sharing experiences.

But this process has often occurred on a political level, and not on a scientific level. The cities we live in are subject to much less documented science than the natural ecosystems that surround them, which we want to protect.

Ildefons Cerdà wrote his General Theory of Urbanization[1] (1867) at the same time that Darwin was writing *On the Origin of Species*[35] (1859). Both texts attempt to demonstrate their hypotheses by making them compatible with the reality they understood and the history that had made them possible.

Cerdà divided his theory into two volumes: one referred to the urbanization process in abstract terms, in a universal sense; the other was a detailed study of Barcelona based on statistical data relating to the container, the contained and the relationship between them, followed by an appendix on the living conditions of the working class.

Years earlier, he had written the *Theory of City Construction*[36] (1859) in which he dealt with the form and analysis of the different parts of a city, where he already considered the air quality in cities or their infrastructures.

From then on, instead of rewriting those documents, all of the proposals undertaken in relation to cities have been promoting the creation of new urban species like Ebenezer Howard's garden city at the beginning of the 20th century, or the Bauhaus modern city, or the CIAM with Le Corbusier at its head in the 1920s.

However, the streets of our cities still have nearly the same section as the streets that Cerdà drew, where he incorporated the water supply, sewer systems, the segregation of wheeled traffic from pedestrian traffic, lighting or street trees.

The Internet has changed our lives, but it hasn't changed our cities yet, as we were saying before. The question remains as to how this change will happen.

During the current transition process, the world's top capitalized companies, the ones that have based their growth on the information economy, some of which have been in existence for less than thirty years, recognize this reality and are preparing to take up "the city" as the direct object of their interest. In fact, this is a great opportunity for cities if they know how to lead the process, if they are proactive and capable of defining what they want.

In an urban economy oriented toward managing services, as opposed to selling products, public-private partnerships are fundamental to the successful management of the city. However, in order for them to be effective, cities should never lose control over their infrastructures and they should define a number of standards that correspond to their aspirations and their specific qualities.

During this transition process, the solution does not lie in increasing the efficiency of an obsolete system through the use of information technologies. We need to rethink the system itself in terms of the new models made possible by information technologies, in order to develop new applications for those systems, which can increase the speed of innovation. In the music world and in telecommunications, this process has already been taking place continuously for years.

Cities, insofar as they are nodes that act as leaders in the transformation of the global economy, need to give up consuming the technologies that industry offers them to become active prescribers of technologies.

Cities don't want to consume what industry has to offer them anymore. Cities want to define new standards to accelerate their reconversion toward more efficient models. As opposed to buying products, they want to engage services. As opposed to installing sensors in cities, they are looking for global partners to help them manage their different infrastructures more effectively.

In some cases, the experience in cities and countries where infrastructure management has been privatized is that the companies come to constitute a parallel state, often putting the shareholders' interests ahead of an interest in innovation and progress. A number of European cities have begun to analyze how to regain control of their infrastructure networks, especially the ones that concern energy, which is central to the new economy for its ties to distributed energy networks and electric mobility. Today, major multinational technology companies offer the same (or similar) products to dozens of cities. They are global managers. However, mayors are still operating on the basis of a purely local vision.

THE CITY PROTOCOL[37]

That is why a new collaborative structure needs to be promoted among cities, with a clear transformational mission, which will allow for accelerating innovation in cites and, by extension, the world.

And, in fact, cities should collaborate with companies, universities and organizations to create a new framework for urban governance. That is why the creation of a City Protocol should be promoted, similar to the Internet Protocol that defines the standards for managing information technologies.

The Internet is governed by an open network. There is the Internet Society, the governmental body, made up of chosen professionals, that promotes the development of the Internet; and there is the

Internet Engineering Task Force, made up of all any experts who want to participate in the debates that take place on open Internet forums, which deal with solutions or recommendations that are used to create the de facto industry standards.

Sharing common standards allows for accelerating the processes of innovation and industrial development. Every city cannot be a world in itself.

If cities share the basic parameters for the challenges they will need to address in the near future, innovation will be able develop faster and will require less investment, because the industry will follow those guidelines, which it has helped to create.

But for that to happen, there has to be basic shared knowledge. Chemistry precisely defines the number of chemical elements and they are classified on the periodic table. In the case of living beings, Carl Linnaeus proposed a classification for all living beings using a number of universally accepted hierarchical levels. In the case of cities, there is no universal classification of the types of urban structures in the world. How many types of districts are there in the world? How similar or different are the extensions of San Francisco, New York or Barcelona? How much embodied energy is there in a sprawling versus a dense city? In order to progress, cities need to share knowledge and define basic, universally accepted principles of urbanity.

The transformation of preindustrial cities has been guided by parameters such as Urban Quality, Habitability, or Accessibility. The transformation of cities in the information society will be guided by parameters such as Resilience or Self-Sufficiency, which are concepts that apply to built cities that intend to offer better stability to their citizens, along with the capability for exercising control. Resilience is the capacity of a city to resist a situation that alters its stability (a fire, a flood, an earthquake, a wave of immigration) and its potential for returning to normalcy as quickly as possible. At a time when climate change is exacerbating atmospheric phenomena that can have a heavy impact on cities, we need to be able to evaluate this new urban parameter with precision, because it is central to associating transformations or investments with a particular territory.

In the past, cities have too often grown in an irrational way. The City Protocol should be a knowledge platform that encourages innovation and progress in cities in the information society. It should allow for the evaluation of the efficiency and the quality of cities throughout the world based on indicators that assess structural, functional, metabolic and social aspects, with the aim of defining projects and policies that will promote progress in the urban habitat in the short, medium and long term.

The City Protocol should be promoted by influential cities, companies and learning centers across the world with the aim of creating standards and recommendations, based on an open and collaborative debate.

Not all cities are alike, in the same way that not all people are alike. There are people who train to achieve excellence by winning at the Olympics or by winning a Nobel prize; both goals involve very different types of training. Not all cities in the world currently find themselves in the same situation; they aren't all heading for the same destination. However, there are basic parameters that all humans need to take into consideration if we want maintain good health, to serve as the basis for achieving excellence. It should be the same with cities.

In cities today, decisions are made intuitively, or according to the logics of the cities that are best organized or that wield more media, economic or social influence. There should be a rational foundation for building a decision-making process concerning cities, which should incorporate multiple levels of information and take into account all the actors that make the construction of the city possible. And at the center of all that, people's quality of life and their social and economic progress should be seen as the ultimate reasoning behind the initiatives that are put into place.

Following the Internet model, the City Protocol should create national organizations to adapt the general criteria to the local cultural and environmental conditions. And it should create sectorial working groups to carry out in-depth studies of the different layers that make up cities.

As such, there should be a record of successful projects that have helped transform one city or another, based on objective data, so that it can be transmitted to other cities in the form of specific information. What kind of economic impact occurs in a city as the result of implementing information networks in public space for the management of its services?

Progress for cities in the information age should be based on sharing information to collectively build a new science of cities.

7. Metropolis
(10.000.000)

Are the world's great metropolises more efficient than medium-sized cities? How can the constant expansion of large urban agglomerations and their interaction with the surrounding natural environment be managed?

Metropolises are the product of urban development throughout the 20th century. Large areas of the territory occupied by a continuous, amorphous, magma. They follow one another, like unconnected pieces, spaces built with different densities and functions, infrastructures and natural spaces, and in order to recognize them you have to go back to a geographical scale, to where the foundational settlements originated.

At the beginning of the 21st century, the urbanization of the world is suffering from a period of perplexity. Never before in the history of humanity have cities been so well understood, yet they have never before been built in such a vulgar way. Cities in developing countries are growing rapidly to house the people who are migrating from the country to the city. Associated with "progress" in their economies, they systematically repeat the errors that Western cities committed in their high-speed growth process. Chinese cities are the paradigmatic example. Extreme zonification (separation of areas dedicated to business, residences and leisure) simplifies the process of urbanizing the territory. It allows for rapid construction of dozens of neighborhoods, at the expense of an enormous consumption of energy resources. Neighborhoods with thirty-story semi-detached housing buildings, which house the workers for hundreds of industrial centers that supply the whole world, managed from huge districts full off office buildings.

The economic logic persists beyond the limits of reason.
The other great superpower of tomorrow, India, seems to be heading in the same direction. As a result, a kind of urban organisms are emerging in Asia that have never before existed in the history of humanity. Organisms where cities of more than 25 million people will have to coexist in coming years and (barring any catastrophe) in the coming centuries, in keeping with new functional principles in the history of cities. In Europe, a district is made up of 10,000 people, a mid-sized city by 1,000,000, and a metropolis between 1,000,000 and 5,000,000, though the largest urban agglomerations in Europe, such as Paris and London, have population of between eight and nearly ten million people. When we are faced with metropolitan areas of 25,000,000 people, it represents a jump in scale that Western societies have never had to manage.

THE DIS-DENSE CITY

On the other hand, in Latin America, the 20th century has created megalopolises of millions of inhabitants where more than 50% of the built surface corresponds to areas of self-building. They are areas where the inhabitants, given the inexistence of consistent economic structures and administrative organizations capable of taking on the housing problem comprehensively, acted in accordance with the basic principle of survival. With as much dignity as possible.

In Mexico City, or in Sao Paulo, one of the most relevant questions in terms of urban issues has to do with the renovation of self-built structures, involving inhabitants in the process of urban transformation. In Medellín, the mayor, Sergio Fajardo, and his team began a process of urban transformation. As opposed to tearing down self-built areas, they connected them with public transportation, improved the quality of public space and built public facilities like libraries and schools. Those are relevant architectural projects, with the aim of promoting the transformation of the city from within, accepting the existence of that built territory as part of the economic and social history of the city.

Every city in transformation has had slums within its limits. In the nineteen thirties, New York also undertook a process to transform its self-built areas. Barcelona absorbed its last remaining self-built areas with the urbanization of the *Avinguda Diagonal*. Bombay and other Indian cities are facing urban transformation processed in which self-built areas, developed with very low construction quality, are disappearing. In Latin America, the quality of these self-built neighborhoods is higher. In many cases the buildings, built with concrete blocks or bricks and between acceptably sized streets, allow for developing the city based on the existing structures.

We worked for the *Empresa de Renovación Urbana* with Willy Müller and Carlos Hernández in Bogotá[38]. With the participation of the sociologist Guillermo Solarte, we studied the transformation of the city centers and other areas of the city. Since I only had two days on my first trip there, we asked if we could see the exterior limits of the city in order to study its center. In no time, they had offered us a traffic helicopter.

It was a fantastic experience because we were able to spend two hours getting to know the different neighborhoods in the city. Bogotá, for example, doesn't have large industrial areas because families carry out a large part of production in their own homes. It is a city that is undergoing significant economic progress, and is promoting the connection between the airport and the city based on shopping centers and the tertiary sector. There are areas of severe degradation in the center of the city, and a process of "controlled demolition" has been initiated, along with the creation of parks in the center of the city and new areas to promote local commerce. On the city limits, mountainous areas are interspersed with rich neighborhoods and developing neighborhoods. The river, located to the south, is contaminated because there is no waste water treatment plant.

As we were saying before, there are different urban clocks within the same city. That makes it very difficult to manage the need for mandatory urban mobility. Millions of people work in places that are very far away from their home and, as such, they are forced to cross the city twice a day for their livelihood.

Every metropolitan area in the world is faced with resolving specific challenges using the potential of technology and the cultural and economic conditions that spring forth from globalization.

DEVELOPMENT IN THE MIDDLE EAST

The Middle East is undergoing an urbanization process similar to the finest hours experienced in Western countries.

What some scientists have described as the zenith of the oil economy has allowed for many Middle Eastern countries to begin the urbanization process at breakneck speed. Their aim is to create new economic structures which will prevent those countries from having to depend on oil for their subsistence in the future.

The development models for Dubai, Abu Dhabi, or Qatar are different, but they respond, once more, to the relationships between territory, economy and government. In 2010, I went to Dubai. It was a few weeks after the opening of the tallest building in the world, the Burj Khalifa, and the sheik Mohamed Al Maktoum's favorite "city," Meydan City, with its operational center in the new hippodrome.

Dubai is an example of this polycentric magma. There is an
unheard-of accumulation of projects with colossal dimensions
set up discontinuously in the territory, like a collage of terrestrial
islands. With projects like The Palm or the Burj Al Arab Hotel,
Meydan City could be the equivalent of the Bilbao Guggenheim. It
is capable of leading a transformation in a built city, which acts as a
magnet for the development of a desert territory which, by default,
is empty. There is only desert.

In Qatar, however, the capital Doha is developing around the
Corniche, where tribes of fishermen (and pearl hunters) used to
ply their trade. A compact city can be clearly seen, which grew up
based on concentric rings, like so many Western cities. However,
on one of its extremes, we find the financial district, which houses
a series of towers (sometimes with spectacular architecture) in a
"non-existent" urban space. The concept of public space doesn't
exist here. The street is just unbuilt space, as opposed to a place
where people can relate with one another, more characteristic of the
new Chinese cities.

In Abu Dhabi, the original growth is also based on the Corniche,
where fifty years ago there were only a few small turrets. They
were used as a control system by the Bedouin tribes in the desert
that operated in the territory. In Abu Dhabi, the capital of the
United Arab Emirates, the urban development has taken place on
the new islands of Saadiyat, Al Ream and Yas. They are home to a
concentration of branches of the most important museums in the
world, along with housing and businesses, with a European-like
urban design. Adjacent, there is the new city of Masdar, with its
Formula 1 racetrack, alongside the Ferrari theme park.

These countries are doing what every country has done when its
economy has experienced growth: they have undertaken physical

developments to create infrastructures and new resources to fuel their economies. Even though the climatic conditions are not ideal for human life. Today, Dubai could be like New York in the nineteen twenties, during a moment of great expansion, when the tallest buildings in the world were being built all at the same time (Rockefeller Center, the Chrysler Building and the Empire State Building). That period ended with the crash of '29 and the Great Depression.

However, building in the Gulf region is the result of a decision that extends beyond the environmental logic of inhabitant a territory in a self-sufficient manner. In the region, people must live with average temperatures of 35 ºC and an average annual rainfall of 107mm. Those atmospheric conditions can only be dealt with at the expense of a significant energy consumption fueled by one resource: oil. They produce it themselves, although one day it will be exhausted on a global scale.

In fact, oil and the wealth derived from it are the reason behind the shape of cities. The presence of multiple relevant projects in Dubai, in many different places, reveals that there is no centralized power that controls the economy and the city, since Dubai does not have large oil reserves. As is the case in Qatar or in Abu Dhabi, the sheiks who own the land are also owners of the oil that can be found underground. Qatar and Abu Dhabi respond to an urban planning that moves beyond the special effects that are characteristic of the accumulation of emblematic projects, which we have seen in Western cities, but Dubai has only expanded at the rhythm of large, pompous gestures.

URBAN NUCLEI

The first metropolis is the one in the film "Symphony of a Great City"[39], made in the nineteen twenties. It shows a Berlin that is just waking up, with the activity of its regional trains and its city buses. A city-machine that works like a productive mechanism where the distances between home and workplace are resolved using a system of mechanized transportation. Metropolises are based on the aggregation of historic nuclei, with one center that heads up the growth. Looking at an aerial photograph of any metropolis, the first thing you see are the geographic elements that dictated the original settlement, which served as the foundation for the city's growth. The island of Manhattan in New York, by the Hudson River, the Seine in Paris, the bay of Bombay or the coastline and the Collserola mountains in Barcelona, define the structure of the territory where the metropolis came into being. And in many cases, the attempt to recognize the limits of the habitable territory reveals natural systems engulfed by the city, which are now part of its urban plan. Some of them are almost natural; others have artificially recreated that nature. The Bois de Boulogne in Paris (846 hectares), or the Pardo in Madrid (15,821 hectares) have the dimensions of urban parks engulfed by the city. Other city have a large-scale natural reference, on or around which the city has grown, but which it has not been able to occupy. At best, the city's growth has been limited. The Alborz mountains in Tehran, or the Guadalupe and Monserrate mountains in Bogotá are two good examples.

NATURAL CONNECTORS

We developed a project in Tehran, in collaboration with the architect Mohammad Majidi, in an area located on the limit between the cities and the Alborz mountains.

The Alborz is an impressive mountain range that separates the plain between Qazvin and Tehran from the Caspian Sea and determines the direction of the silk road. In Tehran, like in many other cities in the world, questions have been asked about the relationship between the city, which has grown from three million inhabitants to thirteen million in recent years, and nature-- in this case a mountain range between 2,500 and 4,000 meters high. For our project, we suggested that the red line that separates the permitted from the forbidden should be substituted by the idea of doors: *The Seven Doors to Alborz* [20]. Seven cultural facilities could be located along this virtual limit, organizing the relationship between the city and the empty expanse of mountains that protects it from the northern winds. Using those seven door, we developed and enclave, defined by a part and a bridge-building, which will house a center for cultural and recreational activities. An element, in fact, that defines natural space as a place to learn about the city. All cities have drawn red lines to define the limit between what is "urban" and what is "nature". Systematically, these lines have been pushed back in favor of the urban areas. Up until the present, human activities, and their habitat, have tended toward growth. If "nature" is understood as the opposite of "urban", as a useless emptiness, its destiny is clear. However, if nature is understood and used as a setting for leisure, relaxation, rest or knowledge, it will serve as one more habitable space.

The limits on growth and on speculation involving land use have led to the creation of self-protection mechanisms. Both the city and what is not the city are defended. But those mechanisms have proven to be ineffective. Urban design, as a discipline separate from the management of the natural environment, seems to have lost its meaning. It attempts to apply techniques for organizing the territory with the main objective of protecting it from us, so that we will value the excellence, inventiveness and innovation in the use and management of the territory.

In fact, the design of nature, or landscape architecture, as Pep Mascaró, the technical director of *Collserola* [40] park, has reminded us, was not part of modern architecture during the 20th century. There were no studies of landscape architecture in the *Bauhaus* [21] school, although they designed everything "from the spoon to the city". For modern architecture, nature was an amorphous space, associated with an abstract kind of leisure, on which isolated housing blocks were constructed, as can be observed in the images by the masters, such as Le Corbusier and Mies van der Rohe. Perhaps the first major modern landscape architect was Roberto Burle Max, a contemporary of Lucio Costa and Oscar Niemeyer, who knew how to integrate nature into the design of cities and buildings.

In fact, the strategic question, in the definition of inhabitable territory and its immediate surroundings, has to do with the interaction between city and nature. And the assessment of which of the two influences the other. It is obvious that, for two thousand years, cities have systematically occupied first the arable land, and then the surrounding woodland. Barcelona, Valencia and many other Mediterranean cities have grown over a very fertile territory, where past generations used to grow the food they ate each day.

In American cities, there has always been a much broader relationship between urban areas and farmland. The dimensions have always been bigger, and the interchanges between cities or "interregional exportations" have been in place from the time the territories were colonized.

At a moment when cities have grown upward and downward, both far and near their habitable nuclei, looking back toward the essential elements of the territory and reevaluating them is fundamental to determining their future development. Especially when it comes to promoting the local production of resources. Recovering watercourses, rivers, the natural systems that cross the territory, or agriculture, can allow for improving the quality of life, increasing the environmental quality, and reducing speed in the operation of nearby systems.

THE OPPORTUNITY FOR RENATURALIZING THE CITY

The Barcelona metropolis is shaped, like few cities in the world, by the natural elements that defined its territorial structure.
The Collserola park is the geographic center of its territorial area. The historical centers of Madrid, Paris or Berlin serve as their metropolitan geographic centers, from which they have grown outward in concentric rings. But Barcelona and its metropolitan urban nuclei have grown up around a number of historical settlements which eventually joined together. Highways and train lines have made daily physical interaction easier between the nuclei that make up the metropolitan area. As such, orography has been a determining factor in defining the expansion of inhabited nuclei. There are now nearly five million inhabitants in the metropolitan area of Barcelona. At this scale, there are infrastructures for water treatment, passenger transportation, logistics, waste management, etc. On the metropolitan scale, we find that the center of Barcelona is occupied by a large natural space, the Collserola park. We see that it is surrounded by urban nuclei and an important system of highways, which trace the limits of the park defined by the Besòs and Llobregat rivers.
Collserola has just been declared a natural park. At the end of the 19th century, when the Eixample was being built, Collserola was

a natural place for Barcelona to expand, with projects related to second homes and leisure activities. The Tibidabo amusement park was built on one of its peaks, which was successful due to the installation of the funicular, which allowed city-dwellers to ride up the mountain. A similar movement happened in places like Montmartre in Paris or the Getty Center in Los Angeles.

The Gran Casino de l'Arrabassada was also built in that period, in conjunction with the urban development of Vallvidrera. Two other urban design projects were also part of that movement toward the top of the mountain, though they had two very different endings. What is known today as Park Güell was a real-estate project developed by the Count of Güell, for which Gaudí carried out the urban design. The project included the construction of individual housing units, only one of which was finally built. Within the gated enclosure, the residents would travel using private transportation. On the northeastern slopes of Collserola, an open project consisting of single-family homes was developed around the Avinguda del Tibidabo. It was served by a public streetcar, and was commercially successful very quickly. Barcelona may feel lucky today that the Count of Güell's project was not a success, due to the collapse of his personal economy and the failure of the development model he chose.

It serves as a magnificent example of the contrast between open projects (like open code communities) and closed projects (proprietary code), which face great difficulties in resisting any changes in the surrounding conditions. Open, hybrid, systems are better adapted to the evolution of the systems that support them than closed systems are.

Years later, the construction in Collserola began to grow. Although it was no longer the wealthy bourgeoisie, but rather the least well-to-do classes. At the time, the bourgeoisie had begun moving northward, toward the Costa Brava or Cerdanya.

In the nineteen eighties, Collserola was marked off as a protected area, with the creation of the first plan based on the idea of transforming the park into public space, cutting off nearly any kind of development beyond preservation.

At the beginning of the 21st century, the park, stretching over more than 8,000 hectares in nine different municipalities, is managed by a consortium directed by a biologist, Marià Martí. It is surrounded by urban nuclei, with an agglomeration of more than three million inhabitants and there are no physical connections with the nearby mountain ranges or the rivers that run beside it.

There are two options in this situation: either the park has the ability to contaminate the surrounding cities, recovering part of the preexisting natural networks, or the cities contaminate the park functionally.

In 2003, a study called *HyperCatalonia*[34], promoted by Antoni Vives who was secretary to the Generalitat de Catalunya at the time, took the opportunity to reflect on the future of cities. At the time, in the throes of urban development in Catalonia and Spain, we studies the rate of acceleration of urbanization in the territory in order to determine when Catalonia would be entirely built up. According to those calculations, all of Catalonia would be urbanized by 2375. As such, it was a good idea to develop a process that could reverse the traditional growth of urbanization in the territory. We proposed the "renaturalization of the territory", a process by virtue of which nature would grow up over cities, engulfing some of the growth from recent years, like residential developments or autonomous industrial areas, creating a new hybrid natural-artificial condition that would serve to structure cities.

After thousands of years of expansion of artificial environments over natural ones, the basic elements of the territory (its geology, topography, botany, climate, etc.) are now the active material capable of action toward creating development in the opposite direction. Those elements can transform historically constructed artificial ecosystems (cities and networks), or create new emergent hybrid constitutions, in keeping with a natural logic.

Collserola's relationship with Barcelona and its metropolitan area proffers this exact same argument. Collserola doesn't need to preserve its natural values; it needs to contaminate the surrounding cities. It needs to recover the structural axes of the natural systems, which are especially visible in the former watercourses in gullies and ravines, and other topographical formations.

In New York the ecologist Eric Sanders carried out a study called *Manhatta: A Natural History of New York City*[41] in which he represented New York before the city was build, with its natural systems and its original fauna. A provocation for rethinking what process cities might undertake in the process toward renaturalization.

The "High Line"[42] in New York is one of the paradigmatic urban spaces in a new kind of landscape architecture, based on visualizing the natural cycles within cities, as opposed to negating them: more in meadows than in flowers. It is a park, managed by a non-profit association, built on an old elevated train line. A park where nature emerges in a wide variety of plants and trees that are characteristic of the meadows in the areas surrounding the city. This renaturalization creates a balance between the medium that houses it and the physical and environmental surroundings.

In order for there to be more nature in cities, there needs to be less use of public space for private mobility.

More nature in cities, opposite building, means lower temperatures in the surroundings and a reduced need for cooling systems in buildings during hot weather.

A city with water in its streets, which recovers old water courses, offers better environmental quality and a more human scale for the city.

NATURAL METROPOLITAN CONNECTIONS

Can the natural networks that have been destroyed by urbanization in cities be connected with the surrounding infrastructures?

After decades of building infrastructures for mobility, logistics and the urbanization of flat land near rivers, we need to give back to nature part of what urbanization has destroyed. In order for an urban space to be natural, the networks that nature needs to house have to be designed and structured technologically.

As a metropolitan project, another of the fundamental strategies to be developed in Barcelona has to do with connecting the Collserola park, currently a green island, with the surrounding natural systems. Especially with the coastal range to the north and the Garraf to the south. To that effect, there is a proposal for the possibility of creating natural bridges to allow for pedestrians, bicycles or horses to circulate through those natural spaces. This would also allow for fauna to move among the different mountainous systems.

The right to travel on foot and the right to a slow pace.

On the other hand, Collserola is also part of an urban system. It is a natural park in the middle of a city and it currently receives more than two million visitors each year. Therefore, as opposed to supposing that visitors will organize themselves, the proper infrastructures need to be created to organize, promote or limit, accordingly, the activities and mobility in the park.

In fact, what we know as forest today, was a very important agricultural space but a hundred years ago. Collserola, like nearly all of the territory, was a space dedicated to the production of food, and wood and energy for the city. Collserola was planted with large expanses of grape vines that were killed off by phylloxera, which destroyed most of the wine grapes in Europe. The territory was structured and managed on the basis of large estates grouped around a number of traditional farmhouses that still exist today. Valldaura, located in the municipality of Cerdanyola, is one of them, founded by the Cistercian religious order in 1150.

NATURE AND SELF-SUFFICIENCY

The IAAC set up a research center on that estate, involved with the self-sufficient habitat, with the aim of learning about how nature works, by coexisting with it. Nature is naturally self-sufficient. It is made up of a series of living elements that take their resources from the environment in which they are established. It can function as a part of a connected whole, as part of an ecosystem. That is what cities should be like.

Up until the 20th century, Man has always interacted with nature through the extraction of resources. While preserving nature at the same time, however, so that those resources were recurrent.

The challenge, today, lies in proposing systems and solutions that allow for the conservation and management of nature, that will be useful in our current context, with the technologies and systems at our disposal.

Cities need to be designed as systems made up of closed cycles for the exchange of energy and information.

During the presentation of the project, we displayed the outline of the project we intend to develop, which is summed up in the idea of "learning from nature through experience". Whereas university education, from the Middle Ages up to the present, has always been based on advanced training in a specific discipline (medicine, engineering, architecture, law, etc.), times of structural change in the world are moments when new disciplines should be invented. They often arise from the hybridization of a number of existing disciplines. One example is biotechnology, the fusion between biology and computation.

We propose taking on multi-scalar education. Centered on human beings and their ability to interact with their immediate surroundings, the objectives would include the local production of resources (food, energy and goods) and the ability to interact globally and share knowledge through information networks.

We need to educate human beings as people and in their capacity to produce the resources they need to live locally and sharing globally the knowledge they accumulate: people, surroundings, planet.

Valldaura[43] will be a multi-disciplinary environment. In 2009, we invited Meg Lowman[44] to Valldaura to teach a workshop; she is the inventor of Canopy Biology, a discipline that studies life in the upper habitat zone in forests, which, in most cases, implies the need for lightweight structures or aerostats to provide access. With Lowman, we undertook a number of studies of the forests and their biodiversity. Valldaura will also be the location for the implementation of the first Energrid network, and where different energy production sources and consumers of energy will be managed using an intelligent network. Energy will be produced there using wind power systems, photovoltaic systems, biogas, biomass and hydroelectric systems.

There is an interesting phenomenon associated with energy because we know what it is, but we don't know how to measure it.

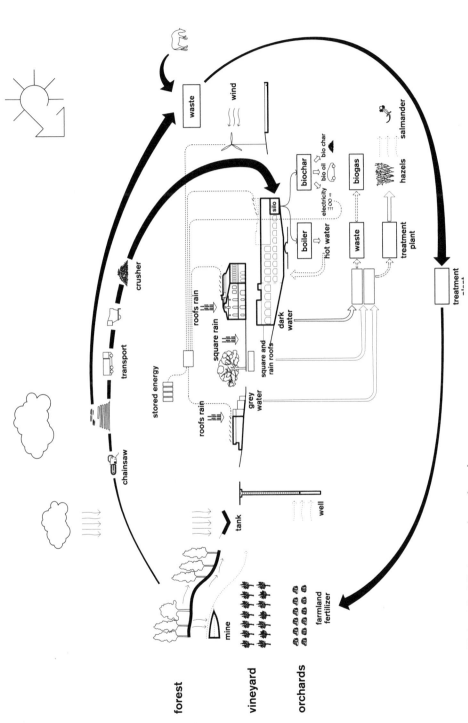

The self-sufficient habitat as a closed cycle

Everyone knows the length of a meter, the weight of a kilo, how fast 10km/h is, how many kilobytes are in an image, but not how much heat a kilocalorie produces. Or how to produce a kilowatt. Culturally, we don't internalize the unit of energy the same way we do with other systems. In order to interact with energy, to produce and consume it responsibly, we should know what it is. And its measurements.

One of the projects that should be developed in Collserola in coming years is the creation of one or more biomass power plants. Each year, the biomass in a forest increases by 4%. If it is not managed by thinning some trees so that the others will grow better, or clearing out the underbrush, it ends up burning or, when it snows, a large number of trees fall, which brings movement in the park to a standstill. Nature evolves through abrupt changes like fires, which are a natural mechanism that allow for spreading trees' seeds, for example. If fires are prevented, people need to increase their management of forestland to promote biodiversity.

Rural activities related with herding, agricultural uses, or the need for energy sources to heat old farmhouses, meant that the wood from fallen trees was collected as a way of obtaining naturally created resources.

But, as many of these activities began to disappear, there was no longer a functional or economic reason to clear the woods and roads, or to pick up fallen trees. That is why the creation of a biomass plant in Barcelona at the foot of Collserola and another on the Vallès side, would create a new reason for clearing biomass from the park.

In fact, the woods are a source of knowledge that the industrialization process has led us to forget. The self-sufficient city should use the resources at its disposal and limit its impact on those places that have the most ecological value. Without giving up on the management of nature and our immediate surroundings, as has always been the case.

HORSES AS INTERFACES FOR RELATING WITH THE WORLD

The integration with nature also has to do with other questions that connect us with ancestral processes and systems.

The world changed when Man learned to tame horses and used them as a means of transportation, allowing for to travel at greater speeds. Horses and their abilities meant that Arab armies could travel faster, and that the heavy Visigoth armies could invade the Iberian peninsula in the 8th century and maintain it for centuries. Horses were our transportation system until the first train was invented and, later, the automobile. However, this animal, associated now with the upper classes, could be a key element in the preservation of the territory.

In the crisis of 1993, I dedicated part of my professional efforts to creating a company that designed graphic interfaces for multimedia systems. In 1995, we won the Möbius prize for the best graphic interface for an architecture CD-ROM[45] at the most important international festival, held in Cannes. In 1997, we were finalists with a product on the metropolitan area of Barcelona, competing against a company owned by Bill Gates that had created an interactive application based on the *Codex Leicester*[46] by Leonardo da Vinci, with a budget that was 100 times larger than ours.

Fifteen years later, in 2008, we decided to learn to ride horseback, with expert endurance riders, which is similar to marathon running and has its global headquarters in Vic. A new way of learning about the natural world. Riding on horseback reconnects people with the earth; you can feel it tremble when you gallop across it.

In the nineteen sixties in Spain, only the most well-to-do classes played tennis. In the wake of the Santana phenomenon, it became a global phenomenon and a large number of tennis courts were put up in residential developments that were being built at the time. In the nineteen eighties and nineties, golf, which was also an elite sport, began to become more popular due to the success of Ballesteros and Olazábal. That was the logic behind the creation of landscapes in a number of urban developments built during those years. In many cases, golf had a harmful effect on the territory, because it is one of the activities that consumes the most land for the least social use.

In the first decade of the 21st century, there has been a boom in equestrian sports in countries like France and Germany and in the Persian Gulf as a national sport. And is hasn't just been horses used in rings for dressage, jumping or racing. Horses are used to travel across the land, which is organized into a sport in the form of endurance races.

In 2007, I met José Manuel Soto, an Andalusian singer who decided to organize the "Dakar of the horse world". It was the longest race in the world, and it was initially called "Al-Andalus". Each year, the race covers 500 kilometers over a period of eight days.

Each year, Soto seeks out 500 kilometers of rural roads in Andalusia for the competitions. We invited him to a conference called "Good News in Urban Design" ["Buenas Noticias en torno al Urbanismo"] organized by the IAAC, because we felt that highlighting the value of the territory by simply racing across it was a great territorial strategy. On the limit between Catalonia and Valencia, I followed the traces of the Roman Via Augusta, which is marked in the Valencian territory. The road was travelled, among other, by King Jaume I during his conquest of Valencia. At present, there are plans to

urbanize that beautiful place and build a real-estate complex.
Near El Puig, where important operating bases were set up, the Via
Augusta is a regional road, fitted out with a series of roundabouts
that dot its length.

Travelling with Soto, I understood that the hope for any rural road
lies in not being turned into a highway. Growth and urbanization
doesn't always represent progress. On the contrary, in parallel to
the network of high-speed trains that cross the territory, we should
build a low-speed network of paths for pedestrians, cyclists and
horseback riders. A network that should have the same normative
value and degree of preservation as railways or national highways.
People have the right to travel the planet on foot.

In a territory of networked self-sufficient cities, the right to walk
or travel, using low-speed systems, and without having to make
excuses to the "king-car", will be one of the fundamental arguments
for the organization of the non-urban territory between cities.

In 2009 I was invited to Princeton University by the dean of
the architecture school, Stan Allen. There I ran into Mario
Gandelsonas, co-founder of the historical magazine published in
New York, Oppositions. Mario told me that he was completing a
study on transportation infrastructures for the 21st century.

"Trains?" I asked.

"No. That was the 19th century," he said.

"Cars?" I asked again.

"No. That was the 20th century," he replied.

"So?" I asked.

"Cell phones and horses." Low-speed mobility with contextual
information that emerges from mobile interfaces.

Incredible.

We traveled along rural roads near *Centelles*, close to Barcelona;
I visited *Mas Cerdà*, which belonged to the family of Ildefons
Cerdà, the engineer with a utopian vision for the construction of
the human habitat, who promoted the idea of "urbanizing" the
countryside and "ruralizing" the city. And he invented the concept
of urban design.
One hundred and fifty years later, we need to rewrite the history of
human habitats.

METROPOLISES THAT ARE INVISIBLE TO THEIR INHABITANTS

Metropolises are the prototype of the industrial city. Large
concentrations of structures and resources in the territory to
satisfy the needs of a large quantity of population concentrated in
proximity to large production centers. These large metropolises are
supplied according to the industrial logic, using energy created in
major productive nodes, like nuclear power plants or wind farms.
In spite of the fact that they are surrounded by what used to be
productive agricultural territory, their food comes from anywhere
on the planet through logistics platforms and transported by sea or
on trains and trucks.
Large urban agglomerations work like abstract machines in
which the brand of a territorial node is promoted as an argument
for competitiveness in the global market. However, most
neighborhoods where people live do not have their own identity
within the metropolis.
Metropolises exist because they are situated around major global
centers, like airports, ports or industrial production centers, and
near places where political decision making takes place.
In the information society, this process of concentrating humanity
in large cities seems unstoppable. The heat of the big city offers

security in a globalized economy, where farmland requires less and less workforce.

Metropolises reach a dimension in which the city itself is no longer comprehensible. In Mexico City, where more than twenty million people are concentrated, daily interaction within the city's districts is much more important; there is a scale of social activity and a certain sense of a "market". There are people who will never visit a multiple neighborhoods in their own cities.

The great metropolises are organized by layers of mobility where the leaders ride in helicopters and land on the roofs of buildings. On the ground level, security is organized by neighborhoods. Could a metropolis be created by grouping together "slow city" neighborhoods (or the equivalent of districts) into a large city?

"Slow cities" are a movement aimed at promoting higher urban quality based on the creation of a slower-paced lifestyle. It emerged from the "slow food" movement, which opposed global homogenization through franchises.

Cities that wish to be members of the club, founded in Tuscany, can have a maximum population of 50,000 inhabitants.

The metropolises of the future will need to promote urban spin-offs: the creation of communities on a neighborhood or district scale, which will be capable of managing their own self-sufficiency, while forming connections with other nearby districts.

To that end, the nodes that will satisfy the inhabitants' needs will have to be identified at the proper scale. In order for this model to be effective, the managers of these networks of connected neighborhoods will have to make use of the culture of cooperation characteristic of the Internet, which has the ability to collaborate on all kinds of initiative using open platforms, as opposed to traditional culture, based on control and confrontation, characteristic of traditional political parties. Nodes, connections, an environment that stimulates life and open protocols for its governance.

FROM "PITO" TO "DIDO"

In March of 2011, a trip to the United States was organized for the mayoral candidate at the time, and current mayor of Barcelona, Xavier Trias, along with Antonio Vives and a group of people. A meeting was held at the Center for Bits and Atoms (CBA) at MIT, directed by Neil Gershenfeld, with the aim of engaging in a debate about some of the ideas in the program for the regeneration of Barcelona, especially those ideas related to the self-sufficiency of city blocks and neighborhoods and, by extension, the city as a whole. A city model with "slow-paced productive neighborhoods within a high-speed, hyperconnected and zero-emissions city". A new mantra.

First, we visited the CBA, where we looked at digital manufacturing machines, from the scale of nanotechnology to the production of any object, like digital printers or CNC machines.

After the tour, we began a debate. Neil talked about the history of the collaboration between his lab and the IAAC. From the Media House to the Hyperhabitat at the Venice Biennale and the Fab Academy. I used images of Barcelona in my presentation: from the city surrounded by walls to the Cerdà plan for the Eixample. He proposed adding value to the territory using the urbanization process, allowing for healthier living conditions for all of the city's inhabitants. After exhibiting the plan, we presented new strategies and projects that could promote a new process to add value to the territories, transforming buildings, city blocks and neighborhoods into self-sufficient zones, proposing a model for the settlement of networked self-sufficient cities. I have talked about all of it in this text. At the end, Neil asked us to go back to the image of Barcelona when it was walled, and he proposed building a new wall:

"Cities should produce all of the resources they need to function, and they should transform all of their waste materials to produce new materials and new products," Neil asserted.

"How do they produce food?" asked a student.

"Ah, right! Vertical farms are already in development and they will allow for growing food in cities," Neil said. He continued, "Energy can be generated using renewable systems, and goods can be produced using digital manufacturing processes. Cities should allow for the import and export of data, not products. Whereas we now have a 'Products In-Trash Out' model, we should be moving toward a 'Data In-Data Out' model, from 'Pito' to 'Dido'," he concluded provocatively.

The project for the connected self-sufficient city, or the DidoCity, can be one of those situations where a framework for general action is defined and a platform is created for the convergence of multiple disciplines and multiple initiatives in the areas of energy production, materials, waste management, communications, recycling and food. An initiative spearheaded by engineers, architects, anthropologists, politicians, ecologists and a wide variety of experts who are essential to defining new paradigms for cities, in order to improve the inhabitants' quality of life with the use of contemporary cultural and technological potential.

EPILOGUE:

FROM METAPOLIS TO HYPERHABITAT

A metapolis is a discontinuous metropolis. A territory organized in a network, made up of urban nuclei, natural spaces and networks that run across the territory. It is the effective space where inhabitants live, work and rest, connected by information networks and transportation systems, and which extends beyond the traditional limits of their dwelling, building, city block, neighborhood, or city.

In his book *Métapolis ou l'avenir des villes*[48], François Ascher defined the discontinuous character of the territory we inhabit, connected through information networks.

The size of a metapolis, as happens with self-sufficiency, is defined by inhabitants through their daily activities.

Cultural identities help to define an effective metapolis, the physical space where individuals operate on a recurring basis, although they are not entirely decisive.

In 2003, we completed a study called *HyperCatalonia*[34] at the request of the Generalitat de Catalunya. The goal was to analyze Catalonia's "metapolitan" territory, looking at the territory as a city made up of cities, highlighting its potential and representing the effects of the advent of the information society on the future of the territory and its cities.

Catalonia is similar to Massachusetts in terms of area and population and concentrates twenty percent of Spain's GDP.

 It has eight times the surface area of Denmark and a fifty percent larger population.

During the study, which was presented at the MACBA, we mapped the Catalan territory using new representations and carried out tests in the form of projects, just like steel bars are stress-tested in materials laboratories, by pushing it to the limit using visions that responded to different programs and scales.

At the end of 2011, Spain completed the largest network of high-speed trains in the world. The dream of a country with a centralized drawing had come true, where all roads lead to all destinations by passing through the center. It is a model that was obsolete almost from the outset, which promotes million-dollar investments to connect sparsely populated territories and ignores investments in necessary infrastructures for corridors like the Mediterranean where large portions of the population and the country's productivity are concentrated, in detriment to the entire system.

The model of the connected self-sufficient city proposes a change in scale for the management of reality, where a city, a metropolis, or a metapolis, as the case may be, becomes the essential governing entity for inhabitants, because the key resources they need for their daily lives are produced at that scale.

We live in a world of cities. Cities cover three percent of the planet, they are home to fifty percent of the world's population and they are responsible for seventy percent of global CO_2 emissions. In 2050, seventy percent of the population will live in cities. Dealing with the environmental challenges the planet will face, which are the source of economic and social challenges, has to happen from within cities. The jurisdiction over energy regulations, or the participation in organizations that are central to world politics, like the UN, or to the global economy, like the World Bank, are controlled by States. At the UN Conference on Environment and Development in Rio in 1992, where the Framework Convention on Climate Change was approved, cities participated on the same level as NGOs. The language of cities is different from the language of States. Their direct interests are different too. The way they manage politics and their rhythms are also different. The crisis in North African countries caused a hike in oil prices worldwide in February of 2011. The fires in Russia in the summer of

2010 caused an increase in the price of wheat. National-scale policies are debated through more or less democratic political systems, national revolutions, and transnational agreements, which treat the control of energy, information, raw materials and food as central issues. We have already talked about that in this text. Information technologies allow for new ways of organizing the world, which means territories can depend on their potential; they can be more resistant because they aren't dependent on the global effects that can impact their resources, and they can engage in a more local organization of the world's habitability, which is more consistent with the environmental challenges the planet is facing.

If the global economy is to be organized around cities, which will produce locally most of the resources they need to operate, while they are connected to the world through information networks; if global commerce is to be based on buying and selling information, rather than on trading physical products that have to be transported around the world in containers, then we will need new structures for governing the world. This is the future logic that emerges from the development of information technologies in the world. It is the Internet of cities. It is utopian to imagine that information technologies will improve cities, but that they won't change the way the world is organized. More and more, people tend to feel identified with their local communities. As a result, many of the responsibilities currently held by countries that are fundamentally dedicated to making laws and handing out budgets, aside from the tasks of defense, will tend to be taken up by larger-scale organizations. That is literally what is happening now in Europe.

The connected self-sufficient city changes the scale of governance of the world and is consistent with an organizational model based on the city-state. Self-sufficient cities and regions that are connected in a network, which possess higher governing bodies, like the European Union or the United States of America, and are connected through global coordination platforms, under the global shelter of the United Nations. The numerous organization platforms for cities that meet systematically, like the C40 or the UCLG, with the aim of coordinating their policies and encouraging joint progress remind us of the beginning of the 20th century when there was a need for the creation of the League of Nations to organize international relations. We are now at a foundational moment for the construction of structures to govern and organize the world, intended to guarantee the common progress of cities and, as such, the planet: The United Cities of the World, or The World Assembly of Cities proposed by Benjamin R. Barber in his book *If Mayors Ruled the World*[49]. In 1995, Nicholas Negroponte, founder and director of the Media Lab at MIT, wrote his book *Being Digital*[50], one of the first manifestos of the information society. In it, he asserted that in fifty years, the United Nations would have 2,000 member countries as opposed to 200. Countries, he said, were too big to be local and too small to be global.

Barcelona and Catalonia, and so many other cities and territories, are the perfect representation of a new world that is emerging, organized simultaneously through city-states and continental organizations, if they manage to work toward the creation of a new status in response to the challenges of the moment, in the same way that the French or American Revolutions did, which allowed for the introduction of new values based on human rights at the end of the 18th century.

The self-sufficient city should be built with the quality of life of its inhabitants and communities as the central aim for evaluating its success, based on a technological reindustrialization process in cities, the local production of energy, and a new food culture of proximity with an increased ecological and environmental value.

Buildings, neighborhoods and cities that are transformed based on
new principles for designing the physical environment, which promote
self-sufficiency.

To make this change possible, we need political and social leadership
in the form of organizations or companies that produce their profits
and promote the collective benefit on the basis of on a new roadmap.
Before us, on the one hand, lies the challenge of using our knowledge
to collaborate in the urbanization processes undertaken by developing
countries, especially in Africa, Asia and Latin America, where more
than two billion people will move into new urban territories over the
next thirty years as a result of population growth and migration from
rural areas into cities.

If all of these countries and their new cities are developed based on
the urban models of the industrial economy, global calamity will be
guaranteed.

But, on the other hand, there is the challenge of adding value to cities
that have already been built, through a productive and environmental
regeneration process, using new technologies and new ways of
organizing our lives, which should finally offer city-dwellers with more
leadership over their own lives. As opposed to managing the presaged
decline of the territories that have been central to the construction
of democracy as a way of organizing citizens' lives, which has seen
its prime physical materialization in cities, we need to work toward
reinventing cities based on new principles, rebuilding them on top of
themselves, as has always been the case throughout human history.

Connected self-sufficient cities.

ACKNOWLEDGEMENTS

This book is dedicated to my wife, Nuria Diaz, who has inspired many of the ideas reflected here, and from whom I have learned so much and continue to learn. To my son León, who teaches me every day and who sparks my personal development. In recent months, I have had the pleasure of living in a three-generation household again, with my in-laws. That has connected me to my childhood in Valencia, where every day we gathered ten people around the table, with an age difference of seventy years. Quite a party.

I would also like to express my thanks to the group that makes up Guallart Architects, for all of the knowledge we have exchanged, especially María Díaz, Andrea Imaz, Fernando Meneses, Daniela Frogheri and all of the collaborators in recent years, with whom I developed many of the projects mentioned here. I would also like to thank all of my partners in the various projects for their support and impetus, especially Angel Gijon, JM Lin and Mohamed Majidi, in addition to the representatives of the companies and governments that have promoted them.

To the whole family at the IAAC, which I directed from its foundation until I was named chief architect of the city of Barcelona. Foremost, to Willy Müller, co-founder of the Institute, Manuel Gausa, Marta Malé-Alemany, Areti Markopoulou, Laia Pifarré, Tomás Díez, Lucas Capelli, Daniel Ibáñez and Rodrigo Rubio, who have promoted many of these projects and have helped create a center for knowledge with a vision determined to encourage innovation in the construction of the human habitat. And, with them, all of the students and researchers, as well as the presidents of the Board throughout its history: Felip Puig, Robert Brufau, Francesc Fernández, Javier Nieto, Francesc Joan and Oriol Soler, and all of the Boards. And to the companies and institutions from all areas and political affiliations that have made it possible. They all had a hand in the creation of a new institution that is Small, Independent and Global.

Since the first edition of this book, changes in the government of the city of Barcelona, currently led by the mayor Xavier Trias, have brought me into the role of chief architect of the Barcelona City Council, in the new Urban Habitat department directed by Antoni Vives. I would like to thank them, along with all of the municipal managers and technicians who possess boundless knowledge about city management.

1. Ildefons Cerdà, *Teoría General de la urbanización y aplicación de sus principios y doctrinas a la reforma y ensanche de Barcelona*, (1st edition 1867, Spanish Edition) Nabu Press, 2012, 842 pp. ISBN 13: 978-1278057859

2. Aaron Betsky, *Out there: architecture beyond building. Experimental architecture, La Biennale di Venezia, Mostra Internazionale di Architettura Volumen 3*. Venezia, 2008. "Hyperhabitat" Vicente Guallart, Rodrigo Rubio, Daniel Ibañez.. view: http://vimeo.com/4295249. *Reprogramming the World: Hyperhabitat.*

3. Salvador Rueda. *Barcelona, ciudad mediterránea, compacta y compleja: una visión de futuro más sostenible.* (Barcelona: Ajuntament de Barcelona; Agencia de Ecología Urbana, 2002, 87 pp.).

4. Dipesh Chakrabarty, *The Climate of History: Four Theses. Critical Inquiry. Vol. 35, No. 2* (Winter 2009, The University of Chicago Press, pp. 197-222).

5. Marshall McLuhan, Quentin Fiore, *The Medium is the Massage: An Inventory of Effects is a book.* (Bantam Books, 1967).

6. Vicente Guallart ed, *Media House Project: The House Is The Computer The Structure The Network.* (Actar, 2005, 263 pp.). ISBN-10: 8460908658

7. Neil Gershenfeld, *When Things Start to Think*, (Owl Books, NY, 2000, 225 pp. ISBN-10: 080505880X

8. Marvin Minsky, *The Society of Mind*, Simon & Schuster, 1988, 336 pp. ISBN-10: 0671657135

9. *Spatial Information Design, The Pattern: Million Dollar Blocks*, Columbia University Graduate School of Architecture, Planning and Preservation, New York, NY 10027, 44pp. ISBN 1-883584-50-7

10. Vicente Guallart, *Sociopolis: Project for a City of the Future*, Actar/Architectektur Zentrum Wien 2005, 294 pp ISBN 10: 8495951835

11. Terence Riley, *On Site: New Architecture in Spain*, The Museum of Modern Art, New York, 2006, 280 pp. ISBN 10: 0870704990

12. Jeremy Rifkin, *The End of Work*, Tarcher; Updated edition 2004, 400 pp. ISBN 13: 978-1585423132

13. Lucas Capelli, Vicente Guallart, *Self-Sufficient Housing: 1st Advanced Architecture Contest*, Actar, 2006, 384 pp. ISBN 13: 978-8496540439

14. Lucas Capelli, Vicente Guallart, *Self Fab House: 2nd Advanced Architecture*, Actar, 2008, 416 pp. ISBN 13: 978-8496954748

15. Lucas Capelli, Vicente Guallart , *Self-Sufficient City: 3rd Advanced Architecture*, Actar, 2010, 416 pp. ISBN 13: 978-8492861330

16. IAAC, Vicente Guallart, Daniel Ibañez, Rodrigo Rubio dir, *Fab Lab House*. Solar Decathlon Europe. Madrid 2010. http://www.fablabhouse.com/

17. Berok Khoshnevis, http://www.ContourCrafting.org/ Director of Manufacturing Engineering Graduate Program at the University of Southern California (USC)

18. Benoit B. Mandelbrot, *Fractals: Form, Chance and Dimension*, W.H.Freeman & Company; 1st edition (September 1977), 365 pp. ISBN 13: 978-0716704737

19. Aaron Betsky, *Landscrapers: Building with the Land*, Thames & Hudson, 2006, 192 pp. ISBN 13: 978-0500285381

20. Vicente Guallart, *Geologics. Geography, Information and Architecture*, Actar, 2009, 543 pp. ISBN 13: 978-8495951618

21. Barry Bergdoll, Leah Dickerman , Benjamin Buchloh, Brigid Doherty, *Bauhaus 1919-1933*, The Museum of Modern Art, New York , 2009, 328 pp. ISBN 13: 978-0870707582

22. Hilary Ballon, *The Greatest Grid: The Master Plan of Manhattan, 1811-2011*, Columbia University Press, 2012, 224 pp. ISBN 13: 978-0231159906

23. Ildefons Cerdá, *La cinco bases de la teoría general de la urbanización*, Sociedad Editorial Electa España, 2000, 448 pp. ISBN 13: 978-8481560657

24. Vicente Guallart, Artur Serra, Francesc Solà, *El teletreball i els telecentres com impulsors del reequilibri territorial. La Televall de Ribes*, Quaderns de la Societat de la Informació 5. Generalitat de Catalunya, 2000, Barcelona, 78 pp.

25. Neil Gershenfeld, *Fab: The Coming Revolution on Your Desktop -from Personal Computers to Personal Fabrication*, Basic Books, 2007, 288 pp. ISBN 13: 978-0465027460

26. Dickson Despommier, *The Vertical Farm: Feeding the World in the 21st Century*, Picador, 2011, 336 pp. ISBN 13: 978-0312610692

27. United Nations, *State of African Cities 2010: Governance,*

Inequality and Urban Land Markets, Local Economic Development Series, United Nations, 2011, 276 ISBN-13: 978-9211322910

28. *Plans i Projectes per a Barcelona:* 1981/1982, Ajuntament de Barcelona, Area d'Urbanisme, 1983, 297 pp.

29. Le Corbusier, *Towards a New Architecture,* Dover Architecture, 1985 (1st edition 1923), 320 pp. ISBN 13: 978-0486250236

30. Eric Mumford , *The CIAM Discourse on Urbanism, 1928-1960,* The MIT Press, 2002, 395 pp. ISBN 13: 978-0262632638

31. Jane Jacobs, *The Death and Life of Great American Cities*, Vintage, 1992 (1st edition 1961), 458 pp. ISBN-13: 978-0679741954

32. Maria Gutiérrez-Domènech, *¿Cuánto cuesta ir al trabajo? El coste en tiempo y en dinero*, Documentos de Economia de la Caixa N 11. Sep 2008, Caja de Ahorros y Pensiones de Barcelona, "la Caixa", 2008

33. Jaime Lerner, *Acupuntura Urbana,* IAAC-Actar, 2005

34. Manuel Gausa, Vicente Guallart, Willy Muller, *HiCat: Research Territories,* Actar 2003, 800 pp. ISBN 13: 978-8495951403

35. Charles Darwin, *On The Origin of Species,* Emporia Books, 2011 (1st edition 1859), 320 pp. ISBN 13: 978-1619491304

36. Ildefons Cerdà, *Teoría de la Construcción de las Ciudades Aplicada al Proyecto de Reforma y Ensanche de Barcelona*, Incluido en *Teoría de la Construcción de las Ciudades: Cerdà y Barcelona* (vol. 1), Instituto Nacional de la Administración Pública y Ajuntament de Barcelona, Madrid, 1991. (1st edition 1859), 342 pp.

37. The City Protocol, *The City protocol society* www.cityprotocol.org

38. Vicente Guallart, Willy Muller, Carlos Hernández Correa, *Multibogota: El por-venir de la ciudad discontinua. Una propuesta optimista para la Bogota del siglo XXI,* Alcaldia Mayor de Bogota. Empresa de Renovacion urbana / IAAC, 2011, 699 pp.

39. Walter Ruttmann, Berlin: *Symphony of a Great City* [SILENT VERSION], 1927. Format: DVD

40. Josep Mascaró, Francesc Muñoz et alt., *Collserola. El parque metropolitano de Barcelona*, Gustavo Gili, 2010, 152 pp. ISBN 13:9788425223129

41. Eric Sanderson, Markley Boyer , *Mannahatta: A Natural History of New York City*, Harry N. Abrams, 2013, 352 pp.
ISBN- 13: 978-1419707483

42. Joshua David, Robert Hammond, *High Line: The Inside Story of New York City's Park,* FSG Originals, 2011, 352 pp.
ISBN 13: 978-0374532994

43. Miquel Sanchez i Gonzalez, *El Cister: i al principi fou Valldaura. Santa Maria de Valldaura, 1150-1169,* Ajuntament de Cerdanyola, 2001.
ISBN 13: 978-8495684189

44. Margaret D. Lowman, *Life in the Treetops: Adventures of a Woman in Field Biology,* Yale Nota Bene, Yale University Press , 2000, 240 pp.
ISBN 13: 978-0300084641

45. Vicente Guallart, Nuria Díaz, *Mateo at ETH,* RA CD-ROM 1, 1994, RA CD-ROM 2, *Around Barcelona,* 1996, Producciones New-Media.

46. Microsoft, *Leonardo da Vinci The Codex Leicester Software,* CD.ROM
ASIN: B000A8J6B6

47. K. Michael Hays, *Oppositions Reader: Selected Essays 1973-1984,* Princeton Architectural Press, 1998, 720 pp.
ISBN 13: 978-1568981536

48. François Ascher, *Métapolis ou l'avenir des villes,* Odile Jacob, 1995, ISBN 13: 978-2738124654

49. Benjamin R. Barber, *If mayors Ruled the World: Dysfunctional Nations, Rising Cities,* Yale University Press, 2013, 432 pp.
ISBN 13: 978-0300164671

50. Nicholas Negroponte, *Being Digital,* Vintage, 1996, 272 pp.
ISBN 13: 978-0679762904

Published by
Actar Publishers
New York
www.actar.com

Graphic Design
Papersdoc

Graphics
Fernando Meneses, Daniela Frogheri,
Daniel Ibañez, Rodrigo Rubio

Printing and binding
Grafos S.A., Barcelona

Distributed by
Actar D
151 Grand Street, 5th Floor
New York, NY 10013 USA
Phone + 1 212 966 2207
salesnewyork@actar-d.com

First edition in spanish 2012
RBA editores

ISBN: 978-1-9402910-3-1

A CIP catalogue record for this book is
available from the Library of Congress,
Washington D.C., USA.